Further Praise for

Dandelion: A Memoir in Essays

"*Dandelion* is a kaleidoscopic memory palace that deftly reconstructs, in spare yet elegant prose, the beauty, pleasure, and horror of Black remembrance and Black forgetting, (fictionalized) through the eyes, sensibility, and voice of her mother.... I have seldom found a character simultaneously so exasperating and deserving of good fate."

—Myriam Gurba, author of *Creep: Accusations and Confessions*

"Danielle Bainbridge's unflinching memoir explores mental illness, family, race, and so much more with clear eyes and beautiful prose. An exceptionally moving and powerful book."

John Green, bestselling author of *The Fault in Our Stars* and *The Anthropocene Reviewed*

DANDELION

A MEMOIR IN ESSAYS

ESSAYS BY

DANIELLE BAINBRIDGE

ISBN: 978-1-938841-41-5

Cover and interior book design: Nicole Roberts
Cover art illustration: Nicole Roberts

This book is available in paperback and electronic book format.

Bainbridge, Danielle

Dandelion: A Memoir in Essays

For Amanda, My Sweetest Love a blessing.

Introduction: I think of Jordan

For a week or more after the incident, I think of Jordan. In the small hours of the night. When I cannot sleep. At the ringing of my cell phone's alarm in the morning. When I am anxious and afraid. When I am silent and still.

How quickly it all became "the incident" in my mind. Even now. I find myself wanting to write about it with urgency. Not the kind of urgency driven by violence, and scarcity, and lack, but rather the kind that tries to snatch back a life from the brink of the extinction called amnesia. I don't want this to be forgotten. But even in my urgency, I find that I forget the details as the memories become softer at their edges.

You may not remember his story at all. I mean, how could I expect you to remember one face, one name, one death in the onslaught of human suffering that periodically punctuates our time online? I mourn that fact alongside his passing.

I wish I could remember exactly where I was when I first heard the story. I was probably at home or some other quiet place. It was posted somewhere online with a kind of carelessness for the loss of life. In the video thumbnail, you can see his face, bloated and red, struggling for something (likely air). You can also see the feet of the other passengers as they shuffle around his limp body. The rest of the video (which I refused to watch) shows him being strangled to death by a man on the floor of the New York City subway.

That is the incident.

I do not watch these types of videos anymore and I haven't for years. The type where Black people are killed. I'm sure you know the ones that I'm talking about. They happen so often now I've sadly lost count. As I see it, the videos are supposed to serve a kind of dual function. On the one hand, they seem to be almost evidentiary, a way to say to a disbelieving world, "Yes, this really happened." On the other hand, they are meant to elicit empathy for the slain victims, as if witnessing it with our own eyes somehow makes their suffering real. Because I am neither disbelieving nor lacking in empathy for the dead, I have decided I will never again watch these livestreamed lynchings.

But the day I stumbled across Jordan's story I could not help but pause at the thumbnail and its agonizing imagery. Do you remember him? I know it's hard to remember one name, one story, amid the deluge. I closely followed his story for a week or more until even I was forced to put it down to attend to the next crisis, the next death, the next, the next, the next, the next. For those handful of days it was all I could think about until I could think about it no more. I spent slow days and hours reading stories about Jordan from online news sources and social media. I traced the facts slowly because digesting them took extra effort as the details passed through my body. From my online inquiries over several days, these are the facts of the case as I know them:

Jordan Neely was a Black man yelling at riders on the New York City subway when a white ex-Marine named Daniel Penny choked him to death in an effort to subdue him. Jordan Neely was having an unspecified psychiatric crisis when he died. He had been unhoused in the city and likely untreated for many years. Sometimes he sustained himself by performing on the subway or busking as a Michael Jackson impersonator and singer. He was thirty years old and Penny was twenty-four at the time of the incident. There had been times in Jordan's brief life when others had been violent with him and he had been violent with others, the details of which are added to the Wikipedia page about his death. That is all I was able to glean from news reports online. It is too much to bear and too little to sum up a life. It is too little to remember a body by. It is not enough detail and still too much to know, empty of substance. Full of pain.

There are videos of Jordan's death recorded by fellow passengers that circulated online and on news programs. It took a week for the NYPD to arrest Daniel Penny in Jordan's death.

I am dissatisfied with what I find online. In the days following his death, I see responses from folks on social media ranging from outrage, to pity, to empathy, to blame, and back around again. Every aspect of his life is dissected, from what he was yelling on that fatal subway trip, to his childhood traumas, to his criminal history. Eventually, he disappears from the news entirely, and we move on collectively to the next outrage, the next wound. I get the sense that many people silently believe him to be a less-than-ideal victim because of his past arrests and complex history with violence. Some even go as far as to praise Penny for "protecting" his fellow passengers that day on the subway. It strikes me as deeply disturbing that Jordan was deemed unworthy of any protection. That yelling became a death sentence. There are so few facts about either man online that do not relate to the incident. Between the two men, it is telling that we only brand Jordan as mentally ill and do not think about what may ail the mind of a man like Penny, a twenty-four-year-old former Marine. I cannot get the image of the video thumbnail out of my head. I shudder when I imagine how close Penny was to Jordan, holding on to his neck, feeling as he first struggled and then became deathly still. Why is this action being lauded as heroic and not unhinged? Is that something you do when you are within your right mind?

Months (or was it a year?) before I learned about Jordan, I read in an article that New York City Mayor Eric Adams had signed a bill that made it possible for NYPD officers to detain homeless people or people experiencing mental health crises regardless of if they are an immediate danger to themselves or others. This effort to detain and criminalize the mentally ill and unhoused was met with immediate criticism followed by an even swifter silence. It seems as if there was a certain level of willful forgetting around this violation of dignity precisely because most people will likely never fall into the category of being street homeless or visibly mentally ill. Therefore the logic seemed to be, "Well if this doesn't impact me, then why should

I care?" The other underlying reason could also be that, for all of their initial outrage, most people silently agreed with the law.

Similar to Jordan's story, Mayor Adams's new law kept me stewing for days after I read about it. I couldn't help but wonder: What would happen to me if I ever found myself in psychiatric distress in public in the city I grew up in and around? What would happen if I found myself dissociating on the subway, yelling at strangers on the sidewalk, or in a restaurant/club/bar, or wandering around without anywhere logical to go? Would I be detained? Arrested? Murdered in plain sight of fellow passengers while they recorded my demise on a shaky cellphone but did nothing else to intervene? I do not ask these questions theoretically. I have dissociated on the subway when having a psychotic episode. I have yelled at strangers in a club in New York City while having a panic attack and experiencing mania. I have wandered illogically on the streets of cities, stepping blindly into traffic, while trying to figure out the workings of my own mind. I have cried in public while experiencing a psychotic break and suicidal depression. But I also have two parents in healthcare who helped me to navigate my illness, and I have always had access to psychiatric care since my early teens when I first started experiencing the symptoms of my bipolar depression. I have access to medications and healthcare providers and support systems that allow me to function day-to-day without (too much) fear anymore.

We are taught to be afraid of the homeless and the mentally ill. When those two categories overlap, we are taught to be doubly afraid. Either we look away because we are scared of contact, walk a bit brisker, or look with pitying eyes and think, "There but for the grace of God go I." I have done these things and had these thoughts when faced with the struggles of others. I have walked away, looked away, switched sides of the street, offered food or money, said I don't have cash, and so much more. Once outside of Penn Station a homeless man approached me, muttering quietly to himself. He asked me for some change and my attention, and I indicated to him that I had no money and that I was on the phone. His anger boiled over and he began to scream at me, "FUCK YOU! YOU'RE ON THE FUCKING PHONE AND I'M DYING. FUCK YOU THEN. FUCK YOU!" There was a rhythm and cadence to his outburst as if he had to say the words many times before. I quickly hurried away because I was afraid of his voice, his anger, his tattered clothes, and his lack of control. But I still remember him screaming about me being on the phone while he was dying. I remember how ridiculous my gesturing for him to be quiet so I could hear the phone call must have felt to a man living on the street and looking for food to feed his hunger. But I didn't stay. I ran away.

What if the safety nets I rely on (medication, therapy, family and friends) were absent from my life? Without these resources, I would honestly be scared about what would happen to me. I am sure I have made people afraid when I was in crisis. I made them afraid with my babblings, psychosis, and rage. I made myself afraid during these moments. But does someone else's fear of mental illness need to necessitate Black death?

I want to live.

When we were kids, every once in a while, my father would come up to us and in his usual brisk manner say "Push on your shoes." With eagerness and delight, we would race to the pile of sneakers at the front door because we knew what this ritual meant. Often it was small: a trip to the ice cream shop or a spin around the park on our bikes. But sometimes the adventures were grander in scale. Unlike our mother's pre-planned trips with us to the bookstore or the library (which were also well-loved) our father's trips had an air of spontaneity around them. My favorite times were when we'd end up taking the train into New York City from my suburban hometown. I'd marvel at the press of people on the trains and the smells of urine, sweat, and street food on the sidewalks (The kinds of street food our mother wouldn't let us eat but our father indulged in.) We'd mostly end up in museums and shops, at shows, the Bronx Zoo, or the Botanical Gardens. Sometimes we'd drive our car to the West Indian grocery stores in the Bronx that carried the food from my parents' childhood in Jamaica. The city represented so much for me. It was a space of possibility for who I could be and become once I escaped my predominantly straight and white suburb where, as a queer Black immigrant child I never truly felt I belonged.

It held the potential of home.

A little bit of that wonder naturally dimmed with age, and now with the death of Jordan and Mayor Adams's law. It no longer felt like the city was this capacious space that could hold me, make room for me, make space. It no longer felt as if there was enough air for folks like us. Folks whose minds can betray us and sometimes confuse others and make them afraid. But what about Jordan's fear? What about the fear he must have felt as he wandered that subway, yelling? As he lost his life? Where are the reports of that? I do not have a more eloquent question to ask, because, like all of the living, I do not know what comes next after our lives end. I hope it is a fuller understanding of the universe. I hope it is eternal peace. I hope Jordan is both above and among us, breathing in a way he was cruelly denied in life.

Unlike my cloudy memory of where I was when I first heard Jordan's story, I remember precisely where I was when I read the verdict of Penny's trial. The news reports that this case "divided the city" and will go to trial in December 2024. At the time the trial begins, I am finishing the revisions on my first book of essays about my mental health. Every day, I sit down to write in the same spot at the dining room table and perform the same ritual:

Write a little.

Refresh my search about Jordan's trial.

Write.

Refresh.

Write.

Refresh.

Write.

Refresh.

This ritual goes on for days. Then, all at once, where there were no answers, there's suddenly a verdict: Daniel Penny is acquitted of all charges in Jordan's death. In the court of public opinion, perhaps Jordan is the guilty party. Perhaps his yelling and his begging for food reminded folks of times when they were riding public transit, or exiting the grocery store, or driving down a busy road and noticed an unhoused person.

Maybe it reminded them of their own fear and apathy. Maybe that is why they work so hard to understand what drove Penny to kill and work considerably less hard to imagine what ailed Jordan's heart. I am looking for Jordan and for those who loved him in this life and beyond. One article headline notes that Jordan's father exits the courtroom every day to avoid seeing the video of his son's death replayed over and over again. But no one seems to be working to understand his pain in the way they are working to humanize Penny in the wake of his actions. It comes out during the trial that a key witness for the defense had lied about Jordan hitting Penny before he was placed in the chokehold. The witness goes on to admit that he was afraid he would be held responsible for Jordan's death because he helped Penny restrain him on the floor of the subway.

It seems that every article I see about the trial features the same image of Jordan on the floor of the subway with Penny's arms tightly circling his neck. His eyes are yellowed, bulging, and distant as he stares at some unknown thing just beyond our view. There is no way to know for certain what the last thing he saw was. Another article notes that his uncle used to drive the streets of the city looking for Jordan, hoping to bring him home. He'll never go home. I don't know what home meant to Jordan. I don't know if it was a place of safety and sanctuary. I don't know what drove him to live outside, exposed to the whims of the natural world and human cruelty. His uncle and his father profess to love him. I can't imagine the pain enveloped in that love now, a mourning that will last a lifetime. Grieving under the scrutiny of the spotlight while the public casts judgments on their loved one. The phrase "loved one" strikes me as particularly sad during these circumstances. The phrase is singular, as if the person described is individually special but also part of the never-ending continuum of folks who have been the recipient of someone else's love. Jordan was a loved one. A subject and object of love. And now he is gone.

I don't know much more about his origins now than I did when I first began writing this essay. But perhaps that is for the best. I think that in a story like mine, a story of sometimes debilitating mental illness, there's often a readerly desire for clear, neat, and utterly traumatic origins. Everyone is looking for the metaphorical smoking gun that is pointed in the direction of the "real" root of all of the sufferer's subsequent problems. I recognize for many folks this is the case, and there does exist a moment, a wound, a pain that serves as the urtext of their trauma. And yet, for me, this simply wasn't the case. I have spent years and years in therapy with a variety of healthcare providers, learning to accept the much less titillating truth: my bipolar 1 disorder is the result of some mysterious cocktail of genetics, socialization, and environment. There is no secret subtext or another story, and I discourage the projection of tragic origins onto this book. Sometimes, mental illness just … is. And it has to be allowed just to be. There is no rhyme or reason, no origin, no moment at which everything went wrong. Some of us are just unlucky enough to struggle. Some of us are born with inexplicable and inescapable pains. Aches that we must nurse for our whole lives. It's like a person who is diagnosed with stage 4 lung cancer after never smoking a cigarette a day in their life. I realize now that there is some good fortune in this lack. Life has given me plenty of heartaches but also more than my fair share of abundance. I have lived a bountiful life. I have tried to be good, kind, and fair wherever and whenever possible. And that has included being good, kind, and fair to myself and my story, no matter how impossible that may sometimes feel.

I caution myself against imagining a single tragic origin point for Jordan. His life has already been reduced to an incident. Most of what we know about him begins and ends on the floor of that subway car. I do not want to do this further. We can speculate all we want. That won't diminish the pain of his passing or bring him back from an early grave.

When I first sat down to write this essay it was an ode to friendship, not a memorial to Jordan. It was a way to talk to and about my friends. A way to talk about the life-giving and life-sustaining power of friendship. I set out to ask the people I love, who also love me, a series of questions or prompts. Some of the questions were more benign like, "At what moment did you consider us *real* friends?" or "What is your favorite thing about our friendship?" I wanted this writing to feel warm, like holding a hand in your own and testing its weight.

The other questions I had felt hard and cold in my lungs, like trying to catch my breath after a winter walk. "How could you love me when I hated myself?" I abandoned this project on the principle that you should never ask a question that you don't want to know the answer to, and began writing about Jordan instead. But the first essay remains underneath this one, like a skeletal artifact fossilized in mud.

I have had very specific touch points on my life's timeline when friendship saved me. I do not mean this metaphorically but rather as a statement of fact.

13, 18, 24, 29.

These ages are tattooed on my mind. The age I was each time I needed emergency psychiatric care. I measure my life against these incremental increases of age, against the process of getting older where once I thought I would not. And each time I was taken to the hospital to combat the machinations of my mind it was at the urging or insistence of a friend. Even when I was as young as thirteen years old.

13: P___ swore our school guidance counselor was "cool" and didn't call parents. Thankfully we were both proven wrong.

18: Flying high on unfamiliar alcohol and newfound freedom, S____ rode with me under the whirring noise of the ambulance siren.

24: T____ alerts my parents to what the doctors later identified as a psychotic break.

29: R____ and K_____ deliver me to the psych ER after a second break.

There is a strange rhythm to these dates and facts. It is a rhythm of steady intervals (always five to six years apart). Like most humans I'm instinctively drawn to patterns and repetitions. I try to decipher their hidden meanings. I think if I am honest (which I strive to be) I would say there is sadness and salvation in these figures. I measure them against the substance of my body. I am my own yardstick. These are the times I should have died by my own hand or illness but did not. The roadmap of my history is etched into my palms. The etchings are lifelines and wrinkles.

"Why did you stay with me?"

In the hospital.

Through the crisis.

On the literal floor of the ER.

In the ambulance.

In the room with the padded walls.

On the stretcher.

In the rooms where the doors only lock on one side.

In the palm of my hand where our skins touched.

In the days after I came home.

At home.

In my apartment filled with cigarette butts.

In the small hours of the morning.

Through the tedium of recovery.

Why did you stay?

"Why did you stay with me?"

This is the only question I have returned to without fail. It is the only one from the original failed project that seems to have stuck. It rattles around, unanswered. It laughs and mocks the perceived progress I've made in therapy. Hours and hours and thousands of dollars spent dissecting my insides only to return to the same unanswerable thing. "Why" is the biggest piece of this linguistic puzzle. An abbreviated version of the question would be, "Why ... me?"

"Why … me?" unites the two components that have never truly made sense to me.

I have always been blessed with friendship from, say, age eleven onwards. Lifelong friends. Heart friends. Soul friends. Friends who have been more to me, meant more to me and done more for me than almost any lover I've ever had. Friendship *was* my romance until my thirties when I met my partner. Friendship was where the light in me was permitted to shine, where I found the beauty of love without the obligations of expectation. Friends were (and are) sacred in my world, in some cases even equaling or surpassing familial ties. Maybe it is because I have always wanted the feeling of being chosen. I lacked that feeling with the casual sexual partners and fleeting relationships of my twenties. But friends choose you. And if they are good friends (which mine are) they make you feel honored by that choice. They uplift and support, love and provide, listen and advise. In comparison to my love life, friendship was steady and predictable. It was like the good partner who comes home to you at night and is quick to smooth the sharp edges of living.

But what does it mean to love someone who is sometimes unpredictable and moody, and alternatingly stable and unstable? What does it mean to love someone whose unpredictability is so often closely linked to a desire for premature death?

But although I hold my friends in such high and sacred regard, I have always wondered if they would ever tire of the work it takes to love me. Or rather, someone with a diagnosis like mine.

What does it mean to stay?

In grad school, I heard a faculty member once reflect on the efficacy of trigger warnings. It is an old and now well-trodden conversation about whether such a warning can prevent or avoid causing additional harm. He reflected that when he first started hearing trigger warnings it was in the midst of the 1980s AIDS crisis and rather than serving as a warning to the listener to remove themself from harm's way, it was meant more as an invitation to stay. To stay and listen, even though what was shared would be hard. To stay and struggle together, alongside each other, in an effort for the grand liberation we all claim to seek. I do not know if this is entirely true, but his explanation seemed beautiful to me.

To stay is an invitation. An invitation to work alongside and with and through the pain.

The writing of these essays took a long time. I worked on them from 2014–2024. That's ten years of psychiatric crises. Ten years of self-doubt. Ten years of learning to understand myself. My years of psychiatric dysregulation were even longer (thirteen when I experienced my first symptoms, twenty-nine when I was finally diagnosed with bipolar 1). I measured the expansion of time in the small cup of my hands day to day while I took this journey with myself. I often journal and when I do, I studiously jot down the date, the time, and the location I was in when I wrote the entry. It was a practice I started in grade school (journaling) and college (noting the specifics of the entry). This has created a rather sprawling archive of emotions that I revisit from time to time, but did not rely on entirely for the creation of this book. Sometimes reading my old entries feels like cold, fresh water in the face. At other times it feels like the salty abrasions of an infinite ocean. But what keeping detailed records has taught me, if anything, is when to throw those same records away and to rely on the feelings. I wanted to capture the feelings here. I hope that I have succeeded in some small part.

If you are reading this, I hope that you can stay with me. I hope you can stay in the same act of inexplicable kindness and grace my friends, my family, and my community have shown me through the years.

As I experienced psychosis.

As I came down from manic episodes.

As I returned time and time again to the hospital.

As I learned to forgive myself.

As I learned empathy and love.

Love for myself.

Empathy for others.

Love for others.

Empathy for myself.

I hope you can stay and that someone has stayed with you, in spite of it all. I do not presume to know why you would read this book. I do not know how it came to be in your hands. But I hope those hands will lovingly receive these words and this author who so desperately wanted to die so many times and now is unabashedly clinging to the heartache of life. I want life for you, for me, for all of us.

"Why did you stay with me?" The unanswerable truth at the end of this question is "When you didn't have to?" You could walk away, look away, switch sides of the street, offer food or money, say you don't have cash, and so much more. You could shush me like a child while I begged for some unnamed deliverance from my own mind.

When I think of Jordan and New York City and my mental illness and you all in the same moment it is enough to leave me breathless. I have spent much of my life wanting to be received kindly. I hope that this version of the truth reaches out to you, even if it can't quite cover the distance to reach you. I invite you to stay, to share space with me, to struggle toward that beautiful liberation we all seek.

I often say to the folks that I love that sometimes we don't realize how heavy something we're carrying is until we go to lay it down. This book is one of those things. I just wanted a place to lay it all down. So I laid it all down.

Here.

Strike Through Ghost Light

We survive among ghosts. On the lower frequencies, deep down in our marrow, where our cells live and die and multiply, we sense the heaviness of them. Their clear felt vibrations. The wailing of half-forgotten injury, ancient and misremembered.

Perhaps it is the weightiness of wanting that lures us back to their gaping mouths and outstretched arms. Perhaps it is a selfish longing, never-ending. I do not believe they all come in violence. I do not believe they all mean us harm. I do believe that they are looking for their own peace, regardless of the cost to the living.

* * *

I am sixteen (perhaps seventeen) years old. I am helping my mother to sort through the piles of junk on and around her desk. This is a periodic and unending task in our household: taming the mess of living in the same place for too long. I drop down on my haunches, roughly pulling out a box at random from underneath the piles, careful not to hit my head on the wooden underside of the desk. I dump the contents of the box unceremoniously on the floor. Among the miscellaneous bits and pieces, I find a small wallet-sized photograph of my mother. In the picture, she is not wearing any makeup, her hair is graying at the root, unstraightened, and has been pulled into two severe cornrow plaits. Her dress, while immaculately pressed, is plain and hand-sewn. Her face is straight, Black, and unsmiling. Although I have seen countless photos of this face—a face I am reminded of daily that is close in appearance to my own—I also know my mother. She would never sit for a picture without paying careful attention to her appearance first. Her hair would be dyed and pressed. Her clothes would be thoughtfully chosen, and store-bought. Her makeup subtly applied. This is in line with all of the women on my mother's side of the family. Although they all prematurely grayed in their twenties, I doubt I've ever seen any of their natural hair colors before.

So, when I find this small picture, I am more than a little surprised. Offhandedly, I look up from my position on the floor and say, "Mama, when did you take this?" flashing the small photo in front of her eyes. She stops, stares at the photograph, and says, "That isn't me. That's my mother." This is the first time I have seen a clear picture of my maternal grandmother's face.

That last statement is both true and untrue. It is the face that she shared with my own mother and the face that my mother now shares with me. Countless times I have been called outside of my name down the tinny, hollow line of a long-distance telephone call. "Pea?" "Is this Paulette?" "I thought you were your mother." "Where's your mother?" The voice whose sound I know better than my own. The face I have seen more often than mine. Its edges are imprinted against the heart of my memory. This is the face that I tell you I have never seen clearly before that moment when I was sixteen (perhaps seventeen) years old. Because it is true.

I remember my grandmother through other people's memories of her. I make food from recipes that taste like hers. I am told the bottoms of my feet are fat and flat like hers. The first time I saw a photo with her feet exposed, I was thirty-four. Her toes are angled and slightly crowded like mine, and the feet themselves are long, fat, and flat. This makes me smile when I show my partner. I do not know if I will die very young like her. A fatal heart attack in her fifties. When I found the first photo, my mother was nearing her own mother's terminal age. Grandmother, we both think about you often.

Grandmother, I was once told that you were buried on the day that three years later would become my birthday. But I've checked your gravestone and know now that it was May 6th and not April. Grief made jagged edges around my elders' memories of you. The day you died in a rural district in St. Catherine, Jamaica, my mother was not yet heavy with the promise of her three children, only empty from the loss of you. It was a month before my parents' wedding. I am a girl child shaped in your image, born one month shy of three years after they buried you. They dug up tender earth in your yard to place you gently there. I wonder about those final moments. I am sure that when you felt your heart fail, you were scared. You were surrounded by your husband and some of your children, the ones who hadn't left for foreign countries yet. I am glad you were not alone in your fear. Everyone on your side of the family has a story of where they were when you passed. I call them the "Where I was when Mama died" stories. It strikes me as odd that we use the euphemism "passed" to describe a death. As if the deceased were just stopping by on their way to their true destination. Either that, or they have been relegated to the past tense once their spirits depart.

The photo I found that day was a passport photo for a trip you never took to visit my mother in the US. You are buried in the yard behind Papa's home. It was your home, too. Papa is your husband. I have known him all of my life. He is 102 years old now and full of mischief. Because of his age, we are readying our hearts for his passing. I pray that those same hearts do not give out under the weight of his impending loss. He has become forgetful, his mind giving over to the throes of dementia. The loss of his memories and his mind scare me more than the transition of his once strong but now frail physical body. When we meet in Jamaica in that same rural district for Christmas or summertime, we often sit on the heavy white stone and tile that covers your grave. Both the stone and our skin become dry and bleached or browned in the sun. When I was a child, I would lie down with my stomach pressed flat against the tiles and imagine you dead underneath me. In my imagination, you were hidden away and perfectly preserved. I hadn't learned about decomposition. I did not know then that it was an American superstition to not cross over the graves of the dead. I have walked miles and miles of circles around your grave. The earth there is uneven and familiar to my flat, fat feet. It receives me well each time I return to your home.

I have saved up many questions about you. What was the timbre of your voice like? What secrets did you cherish, tight like a vest and close to your heart? The same heart that betrayed you when it gave out. What brought you deep sadness and unspeakable joy? How did you find the courage to speak that joy? I know how you loved your children because they still recall that love every day. That is a question I will never have.

You were a seamstress. I cannot sew. But I crochet sometimes. My patterns are wobbly, uneven, and simple, each row resembling a crooked smile.

I have never seen the passport photo of you again. Since then, I've only seen six others. In one, you are standing, cautious in the sunlight, guarding your eyes against the bright rays with the back of your hand raised to the level of your forehead. Your whitish palm is turned towards the camera and the sky. The tree in your yard that I have climbed before casts long shadows on your face. My face. My mother's face. Our face. You are wearing a pink, neatly pressed house dress. When I do not iron my shirts in the morning or refuse to shave my hairy legs and underarms my mother is very ashamed. "You look just like you don't come from anywhere!" she exclaims to me and no one in particular, since she knows in her heart that I come from her and do not do well with criticism (a family trait).

In the second photo, you are lying in your coffin at your funeral. Your arms are folded across your chest, your face waxen and bloated with death. My mother finds this picture in the basement one day and cries. We do not know who took it or who would have sent her a copy so thoughtlessly. In the rest of the photos in that set, I see aunties and uncles, much younger back then, framing the crowd. They do not know that they will become my elders one day soon. My father was not there. He never knew you either.

In the third photo you are younger, maybe in your twenties. By that age, you already had three to four children. You are wearing a pretty white dress. Maybe you were on your way to church or some party. Your mouth is twisted into a little smirk at the side as if you are about to say something fresh. At least I like to imagine it that way. You stand next to another woman I do not know, your hand resting gently on the shoulder of a little boy my mother identifies as her cousin.

The fourth photo shows you with your arm around a young girl, my youngest uncle's smiling face captured in the corner of the image, intruding on the moment. The fifth photo shows you again in your pink house dress, the resemblance to my mother so strong as to be uncanny. Your feet are splayed in front of you and you are sitting in a chair in the house where Papa still lives. You are smiling. The final is the small identification card with an image similar, but not identical, to the passport photo from my youth.

Altogether with the passport photo that makes seven photographs. My mother swears there must be more somewhere. We both do not know where that would be.

I have saved many things. I have paintings I painted when I was six. I have letters from friends since I was eleven years old. Poems I wrote when I was eight. Journals I wrote in when I was between ten and thirty-four years old. Two suicide notes I wrote when I was thirteen. I have letters from teachers that were sent home to my parents before I snagged them out of the mail. I have pages and pages of bad high school poetry about every feeling and nothing at all. I have notes that I took the first time I came back from the psychiatric emergency room at thirteen. I have albums of pictures documenting every event on my life's timeline from the day I was born until mere moments ago. I have the wristband and discharge notes from my second trip to the emergency room when I was eighteen. I have every school identification card I've ever received. Ticket stubs and playbills. Mixtapes and school papers (not all of the grades were that good). Old scripts from past performances and videotapes of my shows. Acceptance letters from every college and grad school I got into. Paper copies of standardized test scores. Every award I have won from age nine until now. Journals from after my third and fourth trips to the psych ward at twenty-four and twenty-nine. I have saved them all. Some of them I kept for many years under my bed. I would sleep on my stomach like I used to lie on your grave and imagine they were rolling away from me every time I got closer to them. Some of them were in a large cardboard box in the living room of my grad school apartment. I used the box like an accidental coffee table because space and money were both sparse in those years. I would sit down on it when I was cleaning so I could reach underneath the kitchen table and behind the couch. My friends rested their feet against its edges and set drinks on top of its surface. I did not mind. I was not attached to the box. Later, its contents would travel with me to the office at my first job, stowed safely in the corner in two big clear plastic bins. They sit there, hidden in plain sight, containing all the corpses of my life.

In my mind's eye, the boxes sometimes grow bigger and bigger. They are sealed in white tile and sun-bleached stone. They become bigger than my whole body and bigger than your grave. I have saved the notes of near death and survival, the horrible poetry, the prizes, the letters, the ticket stubs.

I did not save your picture. The first one I ever saw.

I gave it back to my mother that day when I was sixteen (perhaps seventeen) years old, and I haven't seen it since. She says she cannot find it again and I believe her. I gave her back the photo because it did not feel like it was mine to keep. I don't know who it belongs to, but it wasn't me.

I still hear your words and wisdom often. My mother sometimes repeats the things you told her before you sent her to school: "They can take your money. They can take your clothes. They can take your man. But they can't take what's in here." And she taps the side of her head solidly with her two longest fingers.

I write a little every day, or most days. Some of it is for you. Some of it is about you. A lot of it is about me. This sometimes makes me feel uneasy and ashamed of myself because I want to know what killed us then. What's killing us now.

When I was eighteen, I began to write my first play. In it a young Black woman is haunted by the spirit of her dead grandmother who is played by the same actress as her mother. I wrote it for you, about you, about your picture. I do not know if you would have liked my play. I'm not sure you would have liked the story I am writing about you now. In the play I wrote this line. Sidra (I've called the girl in the play Sidra) says this to her mother. She says this to her mother who is so much of how I imagined you.

Sidra: In ninth-grade biology we learned that two living organisms can never occupy the same habitat at the same time. At first, we all argued with our teacher. So she had two girls come up to the front of the room. She placed one chair in the center of the floor and said, "Both of you 'inhabit' the chair." So they each sat down on one half of the chair. And she said, "Nope you're in two separate habitats. Each side of the chair is a different habitat." The one girl sat in the other one's lap. They moved around a bit and switched positions a few times, but every time our teacher said, "Nope those are still two separate habitats. The lap isn't the same as the chair, or the back of the seat or the other side of the chair" or whatever.

Throughout this Mom has been waiting patiently. She has heard this speech many times before.

Sidra: And that *(pushes the letter back towards Mom emphatically)* is what it's like to have a sister. You're both trying to inhabit the same space at the same time, and you never can. One has to kill the other one.

I have lost all drafts of the play now except for this part. Perhaps it is for the best since it was never very good. Most things you write at eighteen aren't very good (at least that was the case for me). It bothers me that I do not know if you would have found this very funny. I do not know why I wanted it to be funny. You might not have liked it at all. You have several sisters, although I have only met two. There was one named Nussie. She drowned when she was a child. She is entirely a mystery to me. Another one I met was so mean no one liked to take her phone calls. They all swear, "The woman never even gave me an icy mint." Her mind faded in her later life as she slipped into dementia before her death. The other one I know is sweet, blunt, and lovely. I do not know her well, but we have sat together side by side on top of your grave before. She touches her palms to the roundness of my face and tells me I'm getting fat. She says that she loves me. That I am a "nice girl." I am told she is the one who is most like you. Her presence is calm and simple.

I am alive and you are dead.

I do not imagine it any differently. But I remember those summers and Christmases I spent lying down across your resting place. I was cool in the shade of a tree that had cast shadows on your face before. My sister and I are torturing the chickens in the yard, chasing them around and feeding them crushed bits of Oreo cookies fished from inside my mother's purse. I lie flat on the white stone with my face pressed down. Soon I will have to go inside the house where you lived, the

house that you built. A small yard in the country in Jamaica.
During grad school in Connecticut, I sit on a box of my secrets.
A cardboard box pressed tight against the wall of my small
New England apartment. Two more in that same apartment
are tucked under my bed, later in the corner of my Midwestern
office. My body has pressed down on the mattress, suspended
over the contents of my life, rubbing up against the times
I should have died and did not. They have become living
mausoleums that I can sleep above, or stash away, or sit down
on, or let my friends and students rest their feet on when they're
tired.

I am resting somewhere between those boxes and your
grave. All of them are filled with the things that remain. I
am resting there in my mind. I close my eyes and even now
sense the long-drawn shadows from the trees. The magnolia
tree is blossoming in my parents' yard in New York. The
breadfruit tree you planted is growing strong by your graveside
in Banbury, Jamaica. The scruffy and sick-looking maple
tree is changing colors outside my fire escape in New Haven,
Connecticut. The trees by Lake Michigan shudder in the winds
of Chicago.

I do not know if I will die very young like you.

I feel healthy and strong most days.

Dismissed

I woke up this morning with one thought in mind: "Get excused from jury duty." I kept on saying it.

"Get excused, get excused, get excused, get excused."

When I went into the courthouse, I was humming it.

And when they made me sign my name on the attendance sheet. "Get excused."

While I looked over the questionnaire. "Get excused."

When I realized I still had to stay for the rest of the sorting process. "Get excused."

When I heard I would be screened for four different cases.

"Excused."

When they called my name with the unfortunate few to head up to the courtroom.

"Get excused."

When they called my name again for roll call and swore everyone in.

"Get excused."

As I raised my right hand.

"Excused."

As I settled into the jury stand.

"Excused."

As the judge presiding began to read the legal jargon, reciting for the potential jurors what would be expected of us as we fulfilled our civic duty.

"Excused."

I look up and see the two white male prosecutors, tall like trees and straight-faced. I see the white male judge presiding. I see the two young defense attorneys, also white men. The defense team looks about fifteen years younger than the prosecutors and I know that I shouldn't be concerned about age, but it matters to me. I wonder if this age difference will impact the outcome of the trial. I wonder and worry and say nothing.

The judge reads the charges. He mentions the dates. I see a Black man sitting. He is the defendant. He is the accused. He is reading a sheaf of documents clutched in his hands. His bald head is graced by the white weaving of a taqiyah, his

face slightly bowed to read his papers. He is still and patient
as the charges are read, as the witnesses' names are called out,
as the names of every person with any connection to the case
are called out. I look at how thin his body is, and I fidget in
opposition to his stillness. It's almost as if his calm makes me
antsy, as I squirm in a chair that barely accommodates my hips.
The judge continues to describe the charges brought forward
by the state. Murder. One man (a potential juror) raises his
hand to say that he knows two of the mentioned witnesses. He
is asked to give their names, and it is noted by all four lawyers.
The defendant rests. The edges of my eyes hurt with the kinds
of feelings I want to express. I am angry with myself. But I still
can't help but wonder if I'll be excused.

I have been in graduate school earning a PhD for six years.
And on this day I feel so far from God, but I am also so close
to graduation. I have to turn in a dissertation just a few weeks
after this day in the courtroom. And I am worried that I will
miss my four out-of-town interviews for tenure track jobs if they
make me stay.

I have already delayed my jury duty three times. I missed
every date because I was too busy working. Like most
Americans, I think of jury duty as a minor inconvenience akin
to filing your taxes or going to the dentist. Never before had
I stopped to wonder about the composition of a jury, or why
it mattered. I write about Black people. I am a Black person. I
dream a lot about Black liberation. This town's superior court
won't let me delay yet again. I had received a letter in the mail
that today would be my last day to come in as a walk-in juror
before I received a fine. I don't want to pay the fine. I don't have

enough wiggle room in my bank account right now to afford any outstanding fines.

I come to the courthouse almost too late to walk in. I have three jobs this semester trying to save up some money for the first time. I have three jobs in three different states. I never thought anyone would let me do this with my life. Be a writer. I still don't think anyone will most days, which is why I feel compelled to work all of the damn time. I am afraid the work will dry up or I will dry up before I am done with my work.

I don't want to make myself precious. I have been in school for six years. Six adult years of hearing, "So when will you finish again?" "Are you finished yet?" "Did you finish yet?" Six adult years of worrying I wasn't doing anything much with my life. And in that time, I had a psychotic break (the real words for a mental breakdown) and I was involuntarily admitted to a psychiatric hospital for a 72-hour hold. It's what they do when they think you are a danger to yourself or when you may be a danger to someone else. As they were giving me my oral sedative I was crying because they took away my notebooks. Notebooks that I thought (in my madness and fury) were filled with brilliance and divine revelations. Notebooks I read later that were filled with circular and illogical repetitions that frightened me. But at that moment in the hospital, I wailed that they had stolen my privacy. The medical staff offered me loose-leaf paper and a stack of pencils in lieu of my books. I offered them my outrage. I wasn't a child, I told them. Children write in pencil on loose pages without bindings. The loose pages felt like the staff were placating me with coloring sheets, similar to the kinds used as children's placemats in restaurants. Without my pens and the covers of my notebooks they had left me denuded of my privacy. They stole my words. But they didn't budge so I left the insulting pencils and loose pages on a table for someone else to clean up, I took my sedatives and medicinal cocktails, I slept and wept and ate the food my parents brought me. Then I went home to my apartment and my notebooks because I had to sit my exams in six weeks. And I pretended for a while that nothing had happened. After that, I almost left this place. This town with its superior court and this school that I gave six of my adult years. But I won't make myself precious because I wasn't the only person I know who almost died passing through this place.

I know of enough others, folks who broke down or people who went needing treatment. The number of them almost fills the fingers on my right hand, excluding the thumb. The thumb I save for myself.

Almost every grad student I know has been to see a therapist at some point while attending this school. Good majorities of the people of color and Black people I meet here are seeing someone, have seen someone, need to see someone, or are looking for someone. "Someone" is the code word we use to mean psychiatrist. We pass around the names of friendly mental health care providers like bootlegs, or the middle school mixtapes you would make for your friends. We always seem to be asking:

"Do you know somebody who is queer positive? Sex positive? Sensitive to issues of trauma? Knows about Black/ Brown trauma? Won't do more harm than good? Listens well? Understands well? Takes my insurance? Accepts cash? Walk-ins? Doesn't need insurance? Won't hurt me? Won't hurt me?"

I see posts like this almost every day in closed group messages and texts threads. Online, offline, or whispered into the shell of empathetic ears at cocktail parties. We're all moving in the same motions, whisper-passing the same questions. We're all drunk at a party and laughing and looking for someone who won't hurt us. Lobbing these questions at each other like pin-less grenades, live and explosive.

I don't want to make myself precious. But I don't think that it's a coincidence that all of the sadness-heavy scholars around me are obsessed with our ideologies. Our ideas. The collection of ideas. The ways that people arrive at ideas. How we form ideas.

Suicidal ideation: a collection of ideas, forming the ideas, coming up with the idea, to kill yourself.

But we are not a uniquely sad bunch. We are not the holders of ideas, just a group of anxious translators. And as a result, we're all concentrated in fixed areas called Universities screaming our babblings of desperation up to God, if God looked like red wine and vodka and whatever else. I know so many sad insomniacs. Corralled under a shared roof. But let's not be precious. Lots of folks are hurting somewhere. We are just some of the folks hurting on the never-ending spectrum of sadness. We are hurting more than some and much less than most.

I don't want to make myself precious, but I never thought I would finish this whole degree thing. I figured I wasn't as smart as I wanted to be, or as capable as I ought to be, and that not finishing a PhD would have to be all right. Because Black girls with psychotic breaks and bad ideations aren't prime candidates for doctorates (Even though those same characteristics make wonderful stereotypes for "eccentricity" in white male professors and plots for movies about men like that who have inexplicable and brilliant minds.) Plus, the subtle digs really wear down your shit sometimes.

"That's an interesting idea ... I suppose."

"Well it's hard to get a tenure track job. Hopefully, you'll get a postdoc ... at least."

"Careless." "Arrogant." "Oh ... a writer? What have you written?"

And I don't want to make myself precious. But the time I was admitted to the hospital in grad school was the third time I'd been a patient in a psychiatric emergency room. Once for a single day, once for a single night, and once for seventy-two hours. Each time I returned it was against my will. Every time I had to go back the time spent in the hospital got longer. I wondered on the first day of my third trip if I was just destined for lifelong sadness.

But three years after that I am here in the courtroom, at the end of my doctorate, with other ideations instead of my bad ones, and I have four job interviews at places that most people would dream of working. They're not jobs yet, just final-round interviews. But still. I beat out so many people to get into grad school. I beat out thousands to get into undergrad. I beat out hundreds and dozens and dozens to get these four interviews. And I graduate in a few weeks. In the midst of my instability, school was the only constant. I had been trained from an early age to think of education as a contest. I had sacrificed all the years of my twenties to education, and if I wasn't winning anymore, then who was I?

I need to be excused.

I hear the charges read. Charges that will change the shape of this man's life, with his thin Black body and bowed head. I sense his stillness, and I realize that the judge says the crimes mentioned today occurred a number of years ago. And I realize that this man's body, his mind, his ideations have been imprisoned about as long as I've been in school working on mine. And I begin to feel sick inside. Like I hate myself. Because I still want to be excused. But I realize at that moment that I won't try anymore. I won't lie. I won't ask. I think to myself: "You already signed a two-year contract for a short-term postdoc. You don't have to be excused. Maybe you'll get a full-time job next year." Even though in my heart I know this likely won't be true.

"Maybe if you call the departments and tell them you've been asked to serve, they'll let you interview later?" I am too scared to ask.

"This is a man's life. This is a Black man's life. Don't let yourself be excused."

I think of the victim's family. Of the defendant's family. No one is sitting in the courtroom's audience seats except for one steely-eyed and gray-haired Black woman in a pastel overcoat. She looks like she hasn't moved since the moment she sat down. I don't know what she's here for: to show love for the defendant or to bear witness for the victims.

"Don't ask them to excuse you."

I am the only Black woman on this jury panel. I was one of only two in the general pool this morning, back when they were picking out the unlucky few to come upstairs and serve.

"Don't let them excuse you."

I never really believed in the ideology of the court. I don't blindly trust a system with so much horror in it. I dream a lot about freedom, but I don't know how my spirit will receive what I've been dreaming of when it comes. I spend most of my days reading texts about slavery and about why we still need to study slavery. About history and how history can keep on hurting us. I am floating high above my seat in the jury box, dissociated from my body. I think how much smaller a real courtroom looks than the sets on TV. There isn't enough space between the jury box and the judge's seat for the long dramatic crosses in front of the jury box that legal procedural shows love. It's so tight you can barely take two steps.

"Don't let them excuse you."

What of this man's life? What of the lives of the victims? Their families? I think of my family friends who have children who have gone to jail. How it changed the shape of them. I think of a boy I went to school with in the early years of my childhood who was murdered when he became an adult. I think of the people I know through family friends and friends of friends, who have been arrested or gone to prison. I think of justice. I don't fully believe in the court system. I don't believe it's always fair or correct. But not believing in it doesn't mean it will vanish, that it can't harm us. It's still there. I can say I don't believe in cars, but my disbelief won't stop a car from hitting me. The two things aren't equal. And I don't want to make myself precious, but the prosecutors mention the dates of the trial and they have the potential to go on for months and every week this month I have an interview for a place that I never dreamed I could work at.

"Don't let them excuse you."

I am the first one called in for private questioning. The bailiff holds the door open and tells me to watch my step as I enter the witness box, so I won't trip.

I sit down and turn to face the judge. And everything I told myself this morning that I was going to say. Every anti-police, pro-Black, anti-state violence thing in my mind evaporates. I don't believe in the state. That doesn't mean this man won't have his life taken by one. That doesn't mean the victims didn't have their lives taken by one. I don't know what they believe. What the court believes. I want to be free.

The judge asks me, "Is there any undue hardship that you would suffer as a result of serving as a juror in this trial?"

I tell him directly:

"I'm a grad student. I graduate in a few weeks. If I served, I would miss four out-of-town job interviews. But that's all."

I wait patiently for his next question. He nods his head. He asks the four white male attorneys if they have any questions for me. They all shake their heads no in unison. And then I'm dismissed.

One of the attorneys smiles at me a little bit as I walk past and the judge says, "Good luck with all of your interviews." Unconsciously and without artifice I said the one thing that these five men understood. Men who were once in law school, who probably had out-of-town interviews they needed to get to, who had ambitions for themselves and for their careers. These aren't unique ambitions exclusive to these men. But I said something that made them think of my hardship as valid. Something that I never thought would even merit consideration. Giving six adult years away to grad school counted as a hardship in this town's superior court? I didn't have to resort to any form of grandiose ideology. I didn't have to raise hell. They just let me go to my four interviews at places I didn't dream I'd live long enough to work for.

Another bailiff escorts me into the hall. She asks me for my juror badge. I say, "Don't I have to go back to see if they need me for the other trials?" And she says, "Nope. That's it."

I've been dismissed for the whole day. I won't have to serve again for a few years.

I go down the elevator and stand outside. I'm leaning against the pillars of the courthouse smoking menthols. The same brand my high school teachers used to smoke on field trips. The only brand I knew the name of when I started smoking at eighteen. I turn my cellphone back on and I see that I've gotten a fifth interview. At another place that I never dreamed I would go to.

Three years ago (a few weeks after I had left the psych hospital) I was lying flat on the back seat of my parents' car and they asked me where I would dream of working after earning my PhD. Where would I go if I had my choice? And I named the place that had now given me the fifth interview, but at the time I said with a sad undertone, "They probably won't be hiring anyone when I'm ready. And they probably wouldn't hire me."

I smoke two cigarettes outside against the pillars. The courthouse is only a few doors down from my department's building, but I don't want anyone to see how much I've been smoking lately so I stand out there hiding instead.

My godmother told me in my childhood that if you had a dream where you lost your teeth, it meant that someone you knew was going to die. Not too many days before jury duty I fall asleep in the back seat of my parents' car again. Because I've been working three jobs in three states trying to save some money. Because the backseat of their car is where I fall asleep when I'm too tired to talk. Because I've been working to finish this damn degree in a killing place where almost every finger of my right hand is another person I know who wanted to leave here. Because I wanted one of my four fancy out-of-town interviews to turn into a prestigious job but secretly believed they would not. Because I hate myself for wanting things like that. Because the more successful I get at anything, the more my heart learns to love and hate that same thing. Because I have whiplash from listening. Because I am tired. Because I want to have one job in one state in one city, so I don't have to travel so much to make money.

And while I was sleeping, I woke up with a start and spit a smooth hard thing from the inside of my mouth. I looked at my lap where it had landed and discovered it wasn't my back tooth, as I had feared. It was a fragrant piece of sweet guava candy that I had been sucking on before I fell asleep. The kind my mother always keeps in her purse. It must have rolled haphazardly towards the back of my open throat while I was dreaming. But when I spit it out, I swore it was the slick pearl enamel of my teeth escaping through my lips, so I woke up and whispered,

"Who died?"

I Could Only Say Thank You (Part 1)

"Please come home to me." With that (ever so slightly) melodramatic whisper, my mother squeezed me one last time before returning to the car. My father gave me his usual gruff one-armed hug and told me to take care and to "do the right thing." This has been his constant refrain since we were children, as if "the right thing" would always make itself apparent with enough patient vigilance. I exhaled and turned to enter the airport, ready to board a flight to Rome for two months in Italy, working as a stage manager for an American opera company. The fact that I had never met anyone in the company in person, spoke no Italian, and hadn't traveled much in my twenty-three years didn't seem to disturb me at the time. I was gleefully running away with the circus, something I had been threatening to do since early high school. But the truth is, at that point in 2013, I was less interested in running away with the circus and more hell-bent on running away from myself.

Practicality over passion had driven me to enter a PhD program at Yale at twenty-two, right after college. It was practical for several reasons:

First, it was free and after racking up sizable undergraduate debt I couldn't envision paying for another degree.

Second, at the tender age of twenty-two, I didn't have enough creative writing that I was proud enough of to submit a sample to an MFA program. I had pages and pages of bad work that never seemed to go anywhere far. It was mostly circular writing about my feelings and casual observations.

And finally, I had many people in my life, from parents to mentors to friends, telling me that getting a PhD was a "smart" idea for me. It seemed that if I was going to do something as strange as get an undergraduate degree in the arts, then I was also expected to do that in a way that took advantage of my good grades and GRE scores. It wasn't so much that people said these words outright to me. Rather, I inferred this information from their answers. If being a writer seemed like a far-fetched and foreign profession to the people in my life, a doctorate signaled a certain kind of stability and legitimacy. This was in line with what I assumed was the "correct" way to do things after graduation, and so I went to grad school in the fall of 2012. This was before I knew that there weren't many academic jobs left, and the security I would supposedly get from a PhD was quickly becoming a thing of the past.

After an emotionally rocky first year of grad school, I was dreaming more and more of the figurative circus. I missed making art and not just writing about it and its history. When the opportunity arose to join this production as a volunteer, I seized it eagerly and without thinking. I assumed what I would find on the road would be romantic and thrilling and would cure me of what seemed to ail me back in the suffocating college bubble surrounding campus. Living there often felt like a life sandwich with the crusts cut off. And after a year of it, I was desperate for the textures of the crust. I falsely imagined that life as a "real" artist could only begin if I escaped to somewhere where things happened, like New York City. I thought I should be living in a sixth-floor walkup with five roommates, not in my small and mostly barren New England apartment. But I was still convincing myself I had made the right choice and was too scared to let go of my perceptions about what "smart girls" should do with their lives. So, this trip to Italy felt like the perfect opportunity to dip my toes into a life as an artist for the summer, while still clinging to the safety and structure of school. Plus, I still needed my meager graduate student stipend too much to quit school altogether for the great unknown.

During the two months I spent in Italy that summer, I would often joke with the company members that we were actually the equivalent of a traveling circus in the small hillside town where we were staying. What we lacked in death-defying stunts we certainly made up for tenfold in spectacle. Artists from around the world rallied together to brave a series of both bizarre and occasionally wonderful experiences. What follows is the story of that time. The story the stones in the road told me as my feet ate up the earth. The story my eyes told me as they roamed over the skies, hillsides, and faces of strangers. The story my tongue tasted in strange food and my nose smelled in the scents of the air. This story has been told, in part or in whole, before. And yet I feel compelled to tell it again.

∗ ∗ ∗

I arrived in town on what felt like a tidal wave of my own relief. When I stumbled, quite by accident, on the entire company eating lunch in the street in front of a restaurant, I almost shed saltwater tears. When I overheard the faint chatter of English words as I approached them cautiously, I finally unclenched my right hand, which had maintained a stranglehold on my luggage ever since I was reunited with my bags at the airport in Rome. It was, after all, everything I had. In my left hand, I gripped a weathered-looking piece of paper equally tightly. It contained the directions to the theatre that I had carefully printed out the day before (a plane to a train to another train to a bus) and a phone number for our director. Not that the phone number would do me much good without international cell service for my first smartphone. In a moment of peaked anxiety, I had stayed up an extra hour during my red-eye flight to commit the entire contents of this paper to memory like a kindergartener scared of getting lost on their first day of school. When I stood in the crowded airport and train stations en route to my final destination, I took note of the large number of brown-weathered faces asking for change. I only had the big bills I'd just taken out of the ATM and didn't understand the hurried Italian phrases they said to me as they pressed closer. So, I tightened my grip on my suitcase and plowed forward. In town, the company watched as I stumbled by, dragging my oversized bag uphill. I hadn't exactly followed my own rule of never packing more than I can comfortably carry or lift on my own.

A professor in college once told me that Americans traveling abroad behave like Dorothy in *The Wizard of Oz* when she arrives in Munchkin Land. They assume that everyone will look strange and frightening and that the world will go from an orderly black and white to an all-consuming Technicolor. I can't say that I have much of Dorothy in me, but the idea of the "Ugly American" abroad struck me as particularly funny as I set off for my trip. I couldn't truly afford the trip (I'd nearly emptied my bank account and limited savings to pay for it.) But this felt like the right time and place to take a risk.

In the margins of the paper scrunched up in my left hand I had scribbled the spellings and pronunciations of several key Italian words. "Bigletto (Bil-yetto): ticket." "Prego (pray-go): you're welcome." "Grazie: thank you." "Teatro (tee-ah-tro): theatre." I wrote these last two especially carefully along with the name of the town where we were staying. I did not want people to assume that I was dumb, a physical manifestation of a lifelong insecurity.

I arrived in the small town where we were staying without a major incident. I did not get mugged or confused. I didn't get lost. My English (and what I later came to recognize as my American English) seemed to put people at ease. I would smile and say the tentative phrases I had researched online. "Where is the bathroom?" "Can I have a ticket to Roma Termini?" "Where is the bus/train/baggage claim?" Until I reached the edges of the city, far away from the tourist centers, I would usually receive a well-articulated English response.

With great relief, I would lapse into my normal speaking voice (rapid, winding, and rushed) only to discover half the time that the face staring back at me showed little sign of comprehension. The person I was addressing had learned these words and answers for people like me, their English responses serving as a perfect counterpart to my guidebook of Italian phrases. I would acknowledge the moment with a sense of tempered defeat and gratitude and move on to my next location. I felt silly that I could be so crazy as to disembark on such a long trip without the safety of a traveling companion, a university, or any consistent mode of communication. I wondered if people resented my peculiar insistence on speaking English and trying to be understood.

I finally boarded a train that would take me through the Italian countryside, crawling northward from Rome into Umbria. Rushing for the door of the train I was about to miss, a South Asian woman with a crisp British accent and thin arms helped me pull my luggage through the narrow door of the car. I clambered on board, walking down the aisle, searching for a vacant seat. When I finally found one, I looked up woefully at the overhead luggage rack, preparing my overtired muscles to hoist the suitcase up myself. A tall East Asian man stepped forward and, without speaking, easily lifted my burden. I turned to him with my hands grasped in an oddly prayerful gesture and whispered, "Grazie." I assumed he spoke no Italian like me. Perhaps another tourist? When I arrived in town, I realized that this man was our company's tenor. Fluent in Italian, he has lived in Rome for years after migrating from South Korea to study opera. I never indicated to him that we met on the train, but surely he remembers? Something in me is still resistant to mention the circumstances of our informal introduction. Especially to him and even now.

When I arrived at the table outdoors in town with all the other company members, I dropped down unceremoniously into a seat, excited to have found my destination. I lit a cigarette at the table (a habit I started at eighteen that I thought made me look mature, worldly, and writerly that I realized at twenty-nine was just killing me). I was vibrating with excitement. This would be the beginning of something new and I desperately craved new things.

* * *

During my first five weeks when we were based in the town, I did not meet or see another Black woman permanent resident, although I did see five visitors whose presence I closely observe and record. Three women and two girls. None of them stayed for more than one day. Most only stayed a few hours, just passing through on the way to somewhere else.

The first Black woman I saw in town was very drunk and very British. She came staggering out of the hotel next door to the café where my roommate and I were taking advantage of the free Wi-Fi to call anxious families back home. She was laughing loudly and brashly with a white woman who seemed equally intoxicated. Both were middle-aged but dressed in a way that people would usually deem much younger. Short skirts, fitted tops, and smooth-shaven legs completed the look. They looked so powerful to me sitting there with my purposefully hairy legs, plain shorts, and t-shirt, so I watched them as they passed. I assumed they were in town for the wedding that I had seen earlier that day, taking pictures in the square. The wedding party was boisterous and rowdy, spilling out into the streets and going on into the night. But all I could focus on was this woman's dark skin and short straight bob, which paired nicely with lengthy legs sticking out from under a bright blue fitted dress before coming to a point in spiked high heels. How do people walk in shoes like that?

I loved to hear her laughing, striding boldly through the streets of a town where I often learned to make myself marginally less conspicuous or even invisible every day. I loved to watch her take up space. She reminded me a bit of myself when I was at home. Two barrel-chested and stocky white Englishmen in button-down shirts joined her and her friend. I could see from the way that the women spoke to them and the proprietary familiarity of the men's hands that these men were their partners, if not forever, then at least for the weekend. The next day, I saw her again, her eyes covered by the shade of over-large sunglasses in a clichéd gesture signaling a bad hangover. This time, a girl who looked profoundly uncomfortable inside the new height of her lanky frame was walking between the woman and her partner. The girl had a long, curly ponytail interwoven with strands of blond, light brown skin and a sullen face. "She must be their daughter," I thought to myself. I watched them as all three returned to the hotel. I was sitting in the same seat I had watched the mother from the night before.

Second or third week in our small town, Italy I saw a Black mother and her child. Sitting in the plush red armchair of the café with my back flush against a hidden corner of the room where I could easily survey passersby, I saw the girl as she approached. Her skin was light brown, bearing several scatterings of freckles. Her arms and legs seemed impossibly long, her hair an explosion of roots and curls. Her jean shorts had that too-small look, more as if she had suddenly grown taller overnight rather than intentionally buying them short. She crossed and uncrossed her pencil-thin arms, trying to disguise the formation of new breasts and protruding ribs. Despite her gaunt appearance, I felt that she was naturally thin and not sick or malnourished. Yet her skinny frame and general air of ungainliness astounded me.

The mother's skin was a deep dark brown, her hair also pulled into a riot of curls and waves. She had a frowning face. I do not know if it is fair to describe the quality of her face by that one glimpse of her displeasure, but even when relaxed her features had a distinctly *frowning* quality to them. Her t-shirt was a dark color; her shorts were clean and white. I assumed the little girl saw me through the storefront window, although I cannot imagine how.

Immersed in the world of my computer screen, I kept my head bowed, stealing surreptitious glances at their profiles, their shoulders, their hands. I was happy to see them here. While they stood waiting for their order, I heard mother and daughter have a heated exchange in Italian. I could not follow their words. As the argument continued, the mother's voice raised incrementally. Although I did not follow her words, the tone was reminiscent of every mother who feels she has come to the end of her patience and must now correct her child. Her tone said it all: she will brook no argument, she has won, she is right. Finally, with all the energetic antagonism of a teenager, her daughter wheeled around to face me. Pulling her mother by the elbow, they both suddenly rounded the corner and were upon me. With a big grin of satisfaction, the daughter extended her arm fully in a gesture I have become, if not indifferent to, then at least used to: she pointed.

She pointed at me, with my skin and my hair, with my back pressed into the corner. Before she saw me, her mother seemed ready to continue arguing, but when her eyes met mine, she gave me a look of utter disbelief. Her daughter's smile went from victorious to smug as she slowly rotated her face to grin stupidly into her mother's frowning eyes. They collected their order and left, never feeling the need to explain themselves to me.

The last one came to town selling handmade jewelry in the outdoor market. After weeks of hungrily scouring the streets for bodies that resembled my own, I wanted to rush to her all at once. Her short afro and her t-shirt bearing a print of the African continent painted in the Rastafarian colors stretched across her very large breasts and made me think, "She must be an American too." I don't know why but at the time I was convinced this was true.

A friend from the opera company alerted me to her appearance in our little town one morning. Strange how we called this town "ours" after such a short period of time. He had passed her on his way to the café where we always ate breakfast. I was especially happy to see her hair, reaching an inch upward toward the sky in a style similar to my own. She sat in a fold-out chair by her wares and paid little to no attention to me. This made me feel ashamed of my loneliness and of my desire to talk to her. She bartered with passersby in clear, fluent, and rapid Italian. I was going to go over and pretend to be interested in purchasing a bracelet or an earring or anything else in an effort to get her to notice me. To exchange with me. Acknowledge me. Speak Black English to me and not ask to touch my hair like so many of the other people in this town (that's if they asked at all). But I got nervous and shuffled away.

My desire to see myself in a foreign place often baffled me. And yet the desire never dimmed or shifted. For most of my life, I have grown up in predominantly white schools where Black women were scarce, and yet for some reason, the resounding absence of Black women in this remote town struck me as incredibly sad. I craved company that I couldn't find amongst the other artists in our ragtag group. Although we all were coming in from around the world, the stark lack of Black women in the town often made me feel shiftless and uneasy. I could feel people staring at me as I walked to the theatre each morning. Most were too polite to point or comment, but not all were bothered by my obvious unease.

In town, I quickly gained some mild recognition for a few key reasons. First, while several Northern and West African men who came to Italy as migrant workers were living in the town (particularly men I assumed were Egyptian, I would guess to be between ages eighteen and thirty), the town lacked any evidence of their female counterparts. I wondered sometimes about the women back home who weren't with them. Where were they exactly? Were they miles away or living in a town nearby? Did they miss these men? Men who could be husbands or brothers or sons or lovers or neighbors? I often thought about the men working down in the square below my windows in the apartment I was staying in with an Italian host family. To my untrained eye, they seemed to share a bond that I grew to envy in my most isolated moments. My shameful envy was something I couldn't even begin to articulate or explain to myself, let alone to the other members of my company.

I soon realized that they too must be lonely in a country that seemed to embrace Black tourist dollars like mine, while reviling Black and brown migrant labor like theirs with equal amounts of vigor. Although it wasn't synonymous, it reminded me in more ways than one of the US and our relationship with migrants. It was perhaps the most familiar thing I saw in the months I spent abroad.

The second reason I was starting to gain a bit of notoriety in town was that I was the "capo" of the production assistants and volunteer interns. Certainly not the director nor the conductor/composer, who had the ultimate creative control. Rather I was the organizational hub of our group of wandering performers from around the world. Many days and nights I would sit outside of that little café to get Wi-Fi while orchestra members, actors, and technicians clustered around me, clamoring with questions about rehearsal schedules, rentals, travel times, and outstanding payments.

On my first night in town a man who assumed I could understand no Italian pointed directly at me during our welcome dinner and said, "A Black woman boss? How strange." I understand perfectly, surprised at my own comprehension. "Un capo nera? Che strano."

His thick glasses made his eyes look magnified like saucers, his flowing white hair and beard giving him the appearance of a sci-fi wizard or an 18th-century philosopher. This white German expat was our host for dinner. I noticed a young

Black man moving around his house helping to set up the plates before taking a portion of his supper and being sent to eat inside. I learned later that he did not work for the family, as I had assumed, but was actually this man's adopted son. I wondered why he was asked to eat inside. A few minutes later I purposely scared at least three years off of this man's life when I laughed at a joke he made in Italian. The joke was not particularly funny (at least from what I could gather from it), but the antagonist in me wanted him to know that I had understood his previously insensitive comments.

Squinting at me through his large round frames, he had asked me how I had understood. I had said that I had studied Spanish and Latin in school and had a decent ear for foreign tongues if I had set my mind to it. He had told me, unprompted, of his time in Senegal, had asked if I had read Roots, and had said I should have gone to Africa before coming to Italy when I had told him I did not know my ancestral tribe. "This trip ... perhaps less important to you. You would not get as much ... as Africa, no?" I had been worried about how he was raising his Black son.

Excitedly, he later had called his son out of the house. He had wanted to see if I could understand when he had spoken to me in Bambara. I had explained that I only understood languages with Latinate roots, and he had been fiercely disappointed. I had not been so magical after all.

The third reason for my recognition was that I was traveling with a group of often flamboyant performers and artists, a sight that naturally invited the gaze of curious bystanders. And the final reason was undoubtedly my appearance.

"I have been touched by many strangers," I wrote to my friend back in New Haven, making light of the fascination that surrounds my kinked and coiled strands of hair. After several weeks of walking through the streets here, I was still somewhat shocked at the attention my medium afro garnered, mostly from white Italian men. It was also the first time I realized that the word "natural" is something of a misnomer for my hairstyle. Although it was in its unstraightened state I still spent time and effort every morning carefully combing and detangling and teasing the strands until they stood up tall. The ritual made me feel closer to my body while I was there, something I began to need desperately. As I was carefully dodging the outstretched hands of strangers, I read online about Minister Kyenge, Italy's first Black cabinet member. While I was in town, members of the far-right Northern League were calling for her rape. They say they wanted her to finally understand what they believed white Italian women suffer at the hands of immigrant workers. With terror, I watched the mounting tensions. TV screens in public places often broadcast news of her being verbally attacked. The opposition called her a monkey. People asked me daily about the heavy coconut smell radiating from my hair cream. As mosquitoes began to eat me alive, I still wore it every day, too vain to let my hair become dry and brittle, even if it would save my skin. I followed the news and began to take new routes to the theatre every day to avoid the grasping fingers of my "admirers" on the edges of my scalp. I told no one.

* * *

One night at the same café that quickly became our home base (after all, there are only two cafés in town), an Egyptian

man approached me accompanied by his friend, a young
Palestinian I had met earlier in the summer. The Egyptian man
was beautiful, and I have always had a weakness for beauty.
His face was quite arresting, and I could tell that he knew he
was handsome. He asked me in halting English the question
I heard so often every day in this tiny walled medieval town:
"You are with the theatre?" I was being flirtatious and bold,
so I said yes, even though I had little interest in him myself.
Sometimes, flirtation is just something to do. He asked me to
introduce him to my white friend, pointing his finger through
the glass window of the café. He gave me his cellphone number
and stood over my shoulder until he saw I had added him on
Facebook using my phone hooked up to the faint Wi-Fi signal
we were picking up in the street. "Troppo bella," he said over
and over again, pointing through the window at my friend.
Very beautiful. Too beautiful.

   I was uncomfortable with his insistence, but eventually
agreed to at least ask her to come to the hotel where he worked,
where he promised we would both drink for free and swim in
the pool with him and an as yet unseen but promised friend
for me. I agreed to ask, although I made no promises about
her response. I felt very dumpy in my denim work shirt and
jeans, sweaty from a day of moving sets and costumes up and
down hard metal stairs on my back like a workhorse. I resented
my friends sitting inside for looking so well-rested through
the window after a day off of rehearsals while I bartered with
a man outside on the sidewalk. I looked to our mutual friend,
the Palestinian man, to translate, but his English was mostly
limited to terminology picked up in the kitchens and tourist
hotels where he worked. I asked him to explain that my friend
has a boyfriend back home that she is waiting for. I was unsure

that either of them understood me. We had spoken several times before, but mostly about the weather, where they called home, and how they felt about living in Italy. Their feelings about the last subject always remained mixed, a careful blend of partial gratitude, sadness, and ambivalence. I noticed that my probing often made them uncomfortable, so we stuck to things that people in their early twenties like to talk about: booze, dancing, food, and music. Before now, we were almost entirely reliant on hand gestures, broken English sprinkled with limited Spanish, smiles, beer, occasional translators, and goodwill. The beautiful Egyptian man (I'm not sure why, but his beauty seems very important here) lunged forward and touched my arm, saying, "You are from Africa?"

I explained that I was from New York. I did not bother to say the name of my suburban hometown since I doubted that he would know it. He grew frustrated: neither of us had enough common language between us to say what we wanted. "No, but your father, from Africa?" I shook my head no. "Your grandfather?" I tried to say that my family is from Jamaica, which seemed completely ludicrous to me at that moment. In the US, this would have been enough to stop questions of ancestry, even though Black Jamaicans are not native to the island. We claim a pseudo-indigeneity that is somehow deepened upon migration elsewhere. That one extra step of removal gives me enough foreign roots not to have to take another step backward into the void left by unknown genealogy when I am home in New York. The Egyptian man on the sidewalk in Italy asked me where in Africa Jamaica was. This was light-years away from the awe I received from the high school students volunteering with the company when I opened my personal email account days before. In a hushed whisper, they said the name of my "home" institution. "You go to *Yale?*" I looked back at the man on the sidewalk and told him baldly, "Yes. My grandfather is from Africa." It was easier to lie than to explain.

The little café we stood outside of is named Café degli Artiste, "Café of the Artist." The owner was an affable and wide-smiling man who loved the chaos of the theatre people. I think we amused him. The establishment was a self-proclaimed "American café" and every morning when we headed there, the interns and technicians always said the same thing, "Meet for breakfast at the American café?" I was surprised one night while I was enjoying gelato to find that the owner also had a love of American music. He played a mixture of Italian language songs and US Billboard Top 40. One night he took an unexpected detour and played the entirety of Bob Marley's *Exodus* album. I listened to every track of the Reggae god in the American café in Italy and felt at peace. But this man on the sidewalk outside did not know where Jamaica was.

He held his forearm parallel to mine so that his wrist was touching my elbow. I looked down at the two brown arms pressed together and felt an unheeded rush at his contact. I didn't even mind that he was manipulating me; I just enjoyed talking to this man for a moment. He then said, "You help me. You and I, we are the same color."

I was taken aback. I looked at his light brown complexion and wavy black hair, his hazel eyes, his nose and lips and eyebrows. I would never have said we were the same *color*. I've never even called myself African. I sometimes felt sorry for this young man and the other Egyptian men I passed every day in the square. Most worked in the sun, laying down a new turnaround on the street below my window. I felt shamefaced every day when I descended from the apartment where I was staying. Our pianist jokingly called it "the villa." The house was very beautiful. I lived with a widowed schoolteacher and her thirty-year-old daughter, with her aging mother-in-law living across the hall. They were wonderful and warm to me, washing my clothes and fussing that I worked too many hours in the day for such a young unmarried woman, stuffing my eager cheeks with four-course meals and taking me on long day trips in their car on the weekends with the windows rolled all the way down.

The men on the street watched me with curiosity as I came and went. I did not want to be overly familiar or invasive. I read the news every night that the situation in 2013 Egypt was getting progressively worse and thought of those men and hoped they didn't think I was being condescending. I was rapt, watching news of glass bottles soaring in high arcs through the air and covered faces choking on dust and tear gas and burning buildings and cars flipped on their sides to expose their inner machinations. I cannot claim at that moment to truly understand his displacement. After all, he was here to find work and I was here as a willing unpaid volunteer. Our subject positions weren't the same. I saw his Facebook posts about liberation, and mine about police violence in the United States. I compared their content, even though I worried that there was a false equivalency happening in my mind. We both wanted to be heard. We both wanted people who look like us to walk down streets absent of errant bullets and tear gas. We both wanted justice. It shouldn't matter that he had never heard of the place that I call home, either in the US or the Caribbean. To the already numerous barriers existent between us I have added yet another: our racial identity. I thought I would be happy for someone to claim me as one of their own but instead, I just felt roiling waves of confusion. I thought I was more elastic than this.

I looked down at our forearms and back up at the face of the Egyptian man waiting for my answer, stunned at the impossibility of it all. My own sense of American colorism makes me resistant to his claims of kinship. I felt as exasperated trying to explain this to him as he felt when I told him I wasn't from Africa. It wasn't that I could not conceive of us both being descendants of the African continent currently engaged in diaspora, or even that I felt we couldn't both be Black. But the word *color* as a site of community didn't seem to ring true to me. Something there refused connection, even when sitting so close. I looked back down on the literal connection of joints, our wrists and elbows aligned, and yet our differences so pointedly marked as to be tangible. I never imagined that even in this moment of physical closeness I could feel any more disconnected from the men who worked in the square below my window.

After that day he sent me many messages, often late at night. I told him my friend and I were not interested in meeting up with him. He approached us both on the street and whispered warmly into the shell of my ear: "My darling you." I stared straight ahead, my face scorching hot while my friend scuffed her shoe against the edge of the gelato stand where we were waiting in line. If he had wanted to speak to me sweetly as a friend, as a fellow traveler, I would have answered him with nothing but kind openness. But I did not want to be his co-conspirator anymore.

I eventually told our mutual Palestinian friend to get him to stop asking me about the woman in our theatre company. It did not matter so much that we were the same color then. We never spoke again, only smiling shyly at each other in the streets like strangers.

After that one night there was no more Bob Marley music. No more voices to remind me not to cry.

The Hospital: The Spit in My Mouth Heals the Wounds on My Tongue

She is and is not me.

She came down with a case of a yellow heart. All bruise blues turn color eventually. Strapped across the chest and bound by the wrists to the bed, she resumed her prayer to some unseen deity that this feeling would remain, tinged in yellow, and never fully heal over again. If it did then she feared she would lose the shape of her. Lose her forms and her edges and become only so much ephemeral essence, nothing but a chest and two wrists tied firmly to the bed.

She was in the bed waiting on a reckoning or a reconciliation. It felt that something should happen that started with the small, cramped taste of *r*. In a dream, her tongue curled and ached against a hunger only sadness and hot white rice can inspire. She liked her flights of fancy plain but with plenty of salt. It is the same salt applied as an astringent to the tender human meat of our shallow wounds, our common lifeblood staunched by its healing corrosion. It renders our cuts dry and sterile and strangely appealingly edible. Isn't that what drives us to suckle our bleeding thumbs with all of the careless instincts of a child?

The feeling of cold air on her genitals will always remind her of the hospital. When she first awoke in the bed, she was aware of a stinging southward draft. She tasted something like the white chalky medications they gave her and the sour alcohol she had given herself the night before. She had not been trying to die last night, as she was somewhat selfishly obsessed with living. But she had just been trying for once: to fit in, to have fun, to be part of a crowd. And this trying, it seemed, had almost killed her.

She bent her knees slightly, as if preparing for a gynecological exam, and pressed the soles of her feet into the forgiving surface of the mattress. She vaguely remembered some of the steps and the ambulance ride between her friends' apartment-style dorm room and here. She had not taken all of the steps on her own. With knowledge that came from a previous encounter with psychiatric care at thirteen, she twisted her body to look for the plastic bag that would contain her clothes and personal effects. Either they would be by the bed or in a locker somewhere waiting for her to claim them on her way out. She found they only locked her things away when she was at a hospital in a poor or Black neighborhood, although her sample size for this hypothesis was admittedly small. Today, she spotted her things neatly folded in a bag on the chair intended for guests with a note on top from the friend who had taken her to the ER the night before, telling her to call him when she got out. From this and from the fact that she was alone in a semi-private room, she concluded that she must be at the hospital closest to her dorm, the one associated with her university. Later, when the doctor sees the note, she tells her in a conspiratorial tone, "That boy who brought you here must really love you." She cries about that silently to herself when she is alone. She pinches the fat of her dark Black body, especially the skin on the underside of her forearms, and wonders despairingly if this can be true. Could he love her? Was love something that she was entitled to as a sad Black girl?

She did not want to think of herself as a fundamentally fragile and damaged thing. She wanted to become something more dynamic than that. Wanted to live in the sun and the shade in equal measure, rather than always trembling in the long cast shadows of her own mind.

There was dried blood covering the entire back of her left hand, including the fingers, and she began to laugh hysterically. Hopefully, the cackling would alert a nurse to the fact that she had to pee. Later, she would find out that the blood came from trying to remove her own IV in the middle of the night. She considered again her bloodied Black hand. The cut had already formed a crust, and she marveled not for the first time at the potential of the physical body to cure itself. To form its own healing against the tenderness.

There was no clear narrative moment, no point at which things had soured. Yesterday she was not in the hospital. Today she was. Again. That was all the narrative she felt entitled to. She remembered bright flashes of how she'd arrived here, most of the alcohol-infused night blacked out from the recesses of her mind. When she met her friends later to reclaim the things she left behind at the party they whispered that there was "nothing to forgive" and she gave them the love that she couldn't give herself in the moment when she had woken up strapped down to the bed. They still loved her, so she gave them their due. Friends are like that sometimes. They forgive and don't ask questions. Granted, they probably remember more of that night than she does, but she feels grateful to them for their lack of probing and open arms.

She is always amazed at people's capacity to forgive her. Once she had a fever and needed to go to the emergency room. Her throat was so sore and swollen she could barely whisper the words "doctor" and a researched address to the Middle Eastern cabby she found on the side of the road. He was waiting in line for his lunch at a cart and on seeing her slightly delirious state he abandoned his meal to guide her by the elbow to his parked car. Helping her into the back seat, he laid her down across the vinyl like a child and all she had the energy to do was allow it. She continued to whisper the words "hospital" and the address. He continued to shush her, like her mother would do. Too tired to care where the car went as long as it ended up near the emergency room door where they had medicine to cure a fever and a throat too closed up to allow juice to pass through, she heard his whispered words: "You sick. I take care of you." I take care of you. He gave her his card and demanded that she call him later when they let her out. Hours later she would walk home alone in the winter air, determined not to ask for help again. The blocks became miles in her mind. He had not charged her for the ride.

She was and still is deeply afraid of the frailty of the body, of its inevitable infirmity.

The nurse finally arrives at the hospital with her small tray of food. She balks momentarily at the fact that they serve tuna fish sandwiches for breakfast here, but her white nurse is having none of that. With the sturdy build and matter-of-fact affect of a woman unused to casual laughter, the nurse pulls her upright from the bed and loosens the straps. When she is completely free, she begins to lower her legs over the side of the bed before she is hoisted up under either armpit by the same sturdy nurse and guided to the bathroom. She is humming a tune she learned on her father's favorite radio station as a child, the kind where there's a lot of "ooohs" and "baby baby" repeating softly over and over again. Baby baby, oooh! She doesn't remember the words, but she hums something akin to them over the sound of her steady stream of urine as the nurse with the sturdy affect watches her crouch down to pee into the toilet. She knows she cannot be left alone anymore, not while she's here, or at least until she checks out. So, she starts and stops her pee to the tune of the song, bouncing up and down on her bent knees until the nurse, frowning, averts her eyes.

She returns to her room on the arm of the nurse, leaning perhaps more heavily than she would like to admit on the support of a stranger. When they reenter the semi-private rooms, she slides calmly onto the bed and outstretches her arms for the straps. The nurse shakes her head, leaving her alone and untethered with her morning tuna sandwich. Turning her gaze to the clock on the wall she realizes that morning has already come and gone, and it is now close to 2 o'clock. So, she takes her 2 o'clock tuna and eats it a little less gingerly knowing that the infamous morning after is now behind her. She eats with a steady desire for sustenance if not pleasure. She chews the soft mayonnaise-soaked contents of the sandwich slowly and methodically as if giving time for her spit to further break down the squishy solids held against her tongue.

"This," she thinks gustily to herself, "is dying."

And indeed, it felt like dying to be waiting patiently for a doctor in a spotless white-walled hospital room not so far from her dorm. At night, she often heard the sounds of sirens blaring from underneath her dorm room window, rushing patients in for emergency care. Last night, she had been riding beneath one of those sirens. She couldn't explain it, but somewhere between the softness of the bread and the tenderness of the bed, she felt acutely aware of the life slipping out of her. Everything here felt rounded at the edges with no sharp points to punctuate. And without the sharp sting of living, surely, she must be dying.

The doctor entered the room with her pale skin and nondescript brown hair. She had an unusual air of trepidation for someone in a position of authority. She would later learn from her friend, the same loving boy from the note, that she had thrown up on the physician's feet when they wheeled her in on the stretcher, most likely accounting for the uncharacteristically shy MD. The doctor breaks the silence: "How are you feeling today?" Testing her tongue for the first time since waking, she asks the most pressing question on her mind: "What day is it?" She has skipped days in college before. Called them "writer's isolation" when they were just depression-fueled isolation. The MD replies with a tentative, "Saturday," and she nods her head. She has been blacked out since Friday night, or rather early Saturday morning. She asks assertively for a toothbrush. The MD says she can have one soon. The drinks that tasted good at the party twelve hours ago have now gone stale in her mouth.

She sighs and settles back into the cushioning of the bed.

Now it is six years later, she is twenty-four years old, and another MD tells her that she has had a psychotic break. It feels sharp and stinging in her ears so she will only repeat this diagnosis to herself, in private, when no one else can hear it. Although this is one of several trips to the hospital she has taken since her early teens, this is the first time they have said those words: psychotic break. The flavor of the break is barbed and almost poisonous to her system. She always suspected that depression was her issue, but a break? A break signaled a rupture, something that she was unprepared and ill-equipped to fix. They give her a sedative. It dissolves like candy on her tongue and makes her limbs feel like cloth saturated in water, limp and wet.

"Where are my clothes?" She doesn't know why, but she always asks for them. She needs something to grasp, something to ask for, to hold on to. Some adhesive reality, no matter how small, to help heal the break.

She considered the Black skin of her hands for the first time that day. She had been born an exceptionally sad child. Reclusive to the point of silence until early childhood (and long past the point she had developed language) she felt there had always been a concerted effort amongst those who loved her most to "fix" her. Perhaps this time at the hospital marked her first official break, but it was not the first time she had been made to feel broken. She did not know what scared her the most: the break or the underlying suspicion that she had never been represented by a truly unbroken line.

She felt deeply and profoundly about things that had little or nothing to do with her at all. She felt keenly the death of figures she didn't know, the misfortunes of strangers, the injustice visited on mere acquaintances, and the murders of innocents at the hands of authority figures. She had written a letter upon the death of Maya Angelou.

The letter goes as follows:

* * *

Written 05/29/2014 after the occasion of her death.

In dedication.

Edited 11/19/2014 12:01 PM

Dear Dr. Angelou,

You do not know me and now you are dead. I wept bitterly by myself when I heard of your passing. Although you never went to college, I address you here and now and forevermore as Doctor because that is who you are to me. You are my favorite physician. You mixed me strong medicine with the sure hand of an apothecary, you poured out words that ran haltingly over my outstretched tongue (Although I was not always prepared to receive you, even with spoons full of sweet sugar.) They spilled down my throat, hot and unfamiliar. I devoured them. I devoured you. I needed you, loved you, worshiped you, admired you, respected you. Perhaps the most important of all these things is that I loved you.

I was a quiet girl child in a house filled high with the chatter of women. My mother and my aunties (Or should I call them my "other mothers"?) recount stories of my childhood now with the kind of gleeful teasing that only averted disaster can inspire. A dark-skinned infant with an enviable head of full hair, I would sit all day in my baby rocker and look out at the world, chanting "Milkee please!" only when I was hungry and wanted my bottle. I looked at the women working and laughing and playing. I looked at the long legs and bright red lips and sure hips of these giants. I scrambled after girl cousins playing rough out in the yard, my small stature and bookish tendencies preventing me from truly joining in. I hung with desperation to the coattails of my big sister, who in my childlike mind was always stronger and tougher than every stick she threatened to beat the other children who teased me with. I held my tongue and my silence close to my heart. I was a silent Black girl.

Until I was three years old, I rarely tested my tongue. I do not know why now, obviously I was too young to understand then. The first "sensible" thing I ever said came somewhere between ages two and three. My grandfather was visiting from Jamaica, and I feel more than remember the weight of his arms around my chubby infant legs. Looking down over the railing of our balcony I see a woman approach, round faced, short statured, and plump cheeked. My mind tells me she is my Auntie Dahlia, so I glance back into the crowded room at

Auntie Dahlia standing by the door. When the woman comes in and I see them side-by-side in the doorway I gleefully shout, "Two Auntie Dahlia!" making what my mother marks now as my first comparison and the end of my baby girl inexplicable silence. My next clearest memory is at age three, feeling the itchy lace trimming of my birthday dress as I stood posed inside of a McDonald's for my father's camera lens. In my later girlhood I enjoyed the shapes of the people and their funny adult grown-up ways. I loved the headiness of my uncles' cigarettes and the warm sugary undertones in the scent of their rum. I liked to make believe I understood the knowing winks they shared and the eyebrows they raised when looking at the women. I was fond of hiding in small corners where I could peer up and out, unobserved and undisturbed.

When you are a quiet dark-skinned girl child in a house full of beautiful articulate women who weave stories with the ease that other people breathe air, life can bring you many challenges. In hushed and whispered voices these same women that I love often wondered if "the baby was dunce" even long after I understood the definition of the word.

Dunce (noun): (Not always affectionate) Jamaican Creole parlance for a person with an intellectual disability. Simple.

At age three I broke the seal of my silence with the edge of my tongue and poured forth all I had been seeing. I described aunties as fat and tall and short and small. I revealed family secrets to uninformed parties. I parroted curse words with the vigor of a seasoned sailor. I asked embarrassing and uncomfortable questions, often without the privilege of privacy. "Mommy, what's an orgasm?" I asked loudly in the doctor's office, my aunt sitting on my other side. I did not understand the word. "Are you going to marry my aunt and be a father to her children?" I tested the new boyfriend (twenty years her junior) gripping my hands on the edge of a swimming pool, staring up at a man who would later become her husband. "Uncle, you look like a criminal." I grilled him at my grandfather's table all while my papa opened his shriveled wizened mouth to exhale peals of boyish laughter. The running joke? "We couldn't get this pickney fi tahk fi t'ree year and now she nah shuttup!" Jamaican Patois words like "feisty," (a mix of feisty and rude) "inquisitive," and "fresh" were lobbed at me more often than my own Christian name. I grew to love my speaking and never turned my cheek to the power of words again. (This last sentiment is a bold-faced lie). As for my family? They were delighted with my chattiness (albeit not with its unintended side effects) and the rest I can happily say now is history.

But where do you enter, Dr. Angelou? Mixer of strong medicines that stretched the untested muscles of my aching cramped-up tongue? I found my silence again when I entered the school arena. Bounced between classes for "gifted" children and teachers who presumed my silence meant stupidity, I quickly fell into that ambiguous category of "potential problem student." My grades were as irregular as the weather: I was equally likely to receive the only A+ on a class assignment as I was to be sent into parent-teacher meetings for reading novels hidden inside my textbooks when I grew tired with classwork I already knew. In fact, these two instances occurred within the same week. I grew scared of the students who teased me. To be honest I was an easy target. Fat. Short. Bookish. Black. Nervous. Silent. In schools filled with skinny affluent white faces I often floundered for footing. My same sister, stronger than any beating stick, found me once in the bathtub sobbing into the drain trying with all the futility of an adolescent heart to fill my basin with saltwater tears. I cannot measure my own suffering, since there are those much worse off than me and those much better off than I am. I say with not a little shame that there are many more persons in the former category than the latter. But in the myopia of the moment, I did not care. I lost my tongue, swallowed it whole, let it fall into the recesses of my empty stomach. I held it there for many years, but it would not be digested.

My father (who was never quite convinced of the "yu tink the baby dunce fi true?" theory and more in line with the "you are NOT shy, you are contemplative and reserved" camp) and my loquacious mother gifted me my first dosages of your words. *I Know Why the Caged Bird Sings.* I heard your song, and I swore you were whispering sweet words just for me, all alone in my bedroom. I turned eleven and discovered performance. Naturally, like breathing clean air and savoring hot food, I returned to you. I came to you with my illness. I wanted to be heard. It was not with a little surprise that my acquaintances greeted my decision to put myself onstage, let alone in a competitive arena. I'm not sure I ever demonstrated any skills that would lead them to presume I would be good. I memorized your scripture, poured over it like the sacred gospel. I dug deep into my Black girl silence, resurrecting the tears spilled in the backyard, schoolyard, classroom, bathtub, childhood bedroom melee. My father stayed up nights he was home and became my first acting coach. My mother made up my face and ironed my clothes before each competition.

Still I rise. Like air, you told me to rise. Up from the pains of history you told me to rise. You made me a swelling ocean crashing against unfamiliar unforgiving shores. You helped me take up space, to suck in the power of my presence and push it outwards into the air. *I rise, I rise, I rise.* Blushing in my Catholic school uniform, standing in front of the man who raised me, I was unable to articulate one stanza in rehearsal:

Does my sexiness upset you?

Does it come as a surprise

That I dance like I've got diamonds

At the meeting of my thighs?

Sexiness, surely, was not my share? Was I, a little fat-thighed acne-covered Black baby, a beauty? Did I deserve the sway of hips, the knowing looks, the playful pats on the behind of my elders? What was this strange mystery of power, of sex, burgeoning and blossoming out of me? I never said those words aloud in earnest until I entered college. You helped me mine for diamonds. You helped me polish gems.

On the pulse of morning.

You gave a new birth to me. I devoured your words. You allowed me to. I listened to your recordings over and over and over again. You were with me at the mountaintop. Danielle the "problem student" bloomed into a woman I could claim with all my heart. The little girl in the tub, scared to nick her finger on the edge of her tongue, gave way all at once to an actress, a writer, a lover, a friend, a sister, a beauty, an intellect that I could claim without shame or compromise. I will not lie. That girl took your words inside the inner caverns of her heart to the psychiatric emergency room. More than once. But that woman also pressed you close against my chest, your beckoning call pulling tight against me like an invisible string wrapped tight around my sternum, directing my desires. You were on the end of that string, sweet doctor, gently tugging me this way and that like a floating kite. You came with me around the world. You came with me to grad school. You came with me everywhere I could go. Every overturned stone bore your image. Every cranny contained your blinding smile. I mirrored my own speaking voice off of yours (I have never confessed this to anyone. It seems only fair now that you are gone that I share this with you.) You existed, for me, somewhere in the ether of my imagination. I was lucky that my physician was always happy to answer house calls.

I heard of your passing on the morning of Wednesday, May 28th. I was standing in a rented house in the Yucatán, a place I never thought I would visit from the confines of my tear-rimmed tub. I was prouder than I had ever been, surer of myself than I can ever remember. I finally felt the woman I've always wanted to be pushing outwards from my center, pressing herself tight against my skin with the intensity of a thousand birthings. I stood in the mirror, strong for the first time, and heard you had passed, and I wept. I wept with my head pressed firmly against the glass pane of the shower, I let myself weep as if I would never stop. Where was my physician now? How could she go? I turned to my Facebook and wrote the first thing I could think of:

My heart will have to learn a new language of longing to miss this phenomenal woman. Her words have nourished me through

some of the darkest struggles and helped me soar to higher heights.
Rest in Power.

And every word of it was true. I wanted to mourn like the
most small and selfish person in the world. In a moment of
blinding fury, it seemed important to me that no one could
claim any part of this sadness. It was mine to linger with, mine
alone to own. I rubbed firm thumbs under grubby eyes and got
dressed. Face repaired with makeup, dress starched within an
inch of its life, I slipped my feet into forgiving shoes and rushed
off to present my writing. If I was aware when I was young and
fat and black and girl and silent how far I would go I would
have run for terror at the potential of falling from such great
heights as self-love and acceptance. I have always had dreams
of mountains but was perilously afraid of the hilltops. I did not
realize then that I could be the mountain. I could tower high
and tall and proud and strong as you, dear Maya. You gave that
to me.

When I returned home for the day something in me
compelled me to write again. I took to my computer one final
time to send you home, to give you rest, to grant you power,
and to rub healing hands over the chaffing gash your passing
left in me. *On the Pulse of Morning.* I placed a video up (in full).
Your voice rang out to me, and I was surprised at how full of
flesh it sounded. How could you still speak so surely and truly if
you were no longer here? Although the morning had long since
passed, I spoke once more to you:

One of the first pieces I ever performed. Dr. Angelou you taught
me about Black women's performance, internationalism, beauty,
feminism, and grace. You showed me how to stand: feet planted,

shoulders back, head high, voice clear. You wove whole worlds with
your words and gifted them to us. I am forever indebted to your
journey. Remembering you today for your quick smile, wit, and
formidable intelligence. I will remember you always for your words
and your worlds.

I could write love songs to your poetry. I could chant hymns about your face. I dedicate this work to you, a woman who ate life's sweets with the spoilage and gulped them both down whole. Thank you thank you thank you kind doctor. I hope someone's taking good care of you now.

All Love All Ways,

Silent Black Girl

* * *

Back in the second hospital room the MDs ask her many questions. She asks herself an equal number of questions about the letter. Eventually they merge into one. "Why did she write it?" "For what reasons?" "What message did she want to convey?" Is she "safe in her space"? "Did she feel like harming herself?" "Anyone else?" She answers the questions neutrally. She writes because she has to. She wants people to know she loves Maya Angelou. She feels safe in her space. She does not want to harm herself. She does not want to harm anyone else. She knows that if she answers right, if she develops a guarded but strategic technique of response, they will have to let her go. The timid MD stammered in the hospital where she woke up strapped to the bed at eighteen: "You were pretty upset ... when they brought you in here." She nods. Although the alcohol has clouded her memory, she remembers she had not wanted to come in. The MD now, six years later, says, "We'd like to keep you here for further … observation." The MD's nervous pausing causes her great anxiety, although nowhere near as peaked as she would have first assumed. Part of her wants to stay, to be observed, to be tested. This is her third trip to the psych hospital and the only diagnosis she's received is the ubiquitous "depression and anxiety." And now the break. But there has to surely be more to it than that? More to this clawing feeling, more to the swings in emotion? More to the unmitigated sadness and the weight gain and loss and the nervousness and the agitation? The paranoia? There has to be more, because if there isn't more, then she is at the mercy of the whims of her body and mind, completely powerless to stop them or to control herself. And that frightens her more than anything. More than the unpredictability of her mental health. More than her fears of being perceived as "crazy." If there isn't more, then she will never have an answer to what ails her, to what causes these fluctuations in mood and stability every few years. And the not knowing is killing her slowly.

At twenty-four, she asks unnecessarily roughly, "How long will I have to stay here?" She says it in a voice that has gone unused for many hours and is hoarse with the effort of articulation. The MD says "One, maybe two days or until you can be safely discharged" before leaving her alone with her half-empty tray of food and her plastic bag full of clothes and her thoughts.

The next two days pass in a haze of routine. She wakes up. She pees. She eats. She watches TV. She eats. She sleeps. She does not interact with many other patients. One tall woman with an imposing frame lives on the floor. Her shoulders span an impressive width, and her voice is deep and growling. She has long dreadlocked hair and skin that looks deeper in color the longer you look at it, a color so rich it is beyond brown. The other woman in her small suite of rooms is a light dusky brown that speaks to mixed heritage. Her own righteous curls spring forth in a million independent directions, and she spends much of her time worrying the ends of her hair between the sticky tips of her fingers. When this woman comes over to play in her hair, curious about its Black girl textures, she remembers a childhood friend who once stood over her making monkey sounds and pretending to dig bugs out of her straightened hair to eat. Both women live on the floor she is staying on and seem friendly but dissociated. Even in her state of unwellness, she can tell this much. Most of the patients at this hospital are Black or brown because most of the people in the neighborhood where the hospital is located are Black or brown. She hears people moaning and crying, screaming through the walls at night. She tries to block it out and get some rest.

The doctors and nurses frequently come to ask her questions. She answers them in a way she assumes is normal and succinct. The day they tell her she can leave she cries a bitter cocktail of relief and disappointment. What is wrong? Why is she here? Will she be back again? Is she healed? Is she now "safe in her space"?

Five years later she is in the hospital again. Twenty-nine, over a decade after she woke up strapped to the bed at eighteen. Another psychotic break, another involuntary hold. This time she is held for five nights and six days. When you stay that long you can sometimes get your clothes back if you act nicely and behave well. So, on the third day, she asks for her bag. She had arrived at the hospital in a tank top with no bra and a pair of jeans. When she emerges dressed in her own clothes the nurses look at her erect nipples and tell her to go put on another shirt. This is all she has, so they return with a nondescript tie-dye shirt and tell her to wear that instead. This stay in the hospital is different because it is the fourth time. By now, she knows the strategies to survive. She wanders the halls, goes to group therapy, eats food that has so much dairy it makes her lactose-intolerant body constipated for four days after she leaves.

The walls of this hospital are gleaming and white, sterile but not particularly clean. She hears people in other rooms groaning loudly at night, losing track of how many folks burst into tears on a daily basis. One night she gets scared and drags her blanket into the hallway to sleep under the watchful eye of a security camera. In her mania, she believes this will keep her safe from the disembodied groans from neighboring rooms. A doctor comes to gently coax her off the floor and back to her bed where she sits up all night for the first two days before they have to hold her arms down and inject her with a sedative to make her sleep. As she drifts off, she can see the light from a police car outside through the iron mesh covering the windows. The red of the lights blurs in her vision as she is forced into a medicated sleep.

When her friend first brings her in at twenty-nine for evaluation, an alarm goes off in the ER. She is scared of the blaring, so she goes to the nurses' station and wads pieces of tissue paper in her mouth, wetting them with spit before sticking the spitballs in her ears. Her friend appears, seemingly out of nowhere, and sits next to her on the floor in front of the nurses' station. Trying to calm her down, the friend takes her head in her cool hands and places it on her lap. They sit there for what seems like hours, rocking back and forth as the alarms blaze. That same day, she refused to change into a hospital gown (She never claimed to be an easy patient.) The white male physician calls in two police officers after she yells at him, which makes her panic and retreat to the corner of the room. The carceral nature of psychiatric care in this country astounds her, and she thinks about that moment often after she is discharged. She assumes the officers were just brought in to scare her into compliance. But hadn't she been scared enough in one day? At the end of her stay in the hospital, she sees the words on her discharge sheet. Written sloppily under "cause for admission," she sees the words "bipolar depression." She is shocked. What happened to "stress" or "anxiety and depression"? These vague diagnoses have followed her since her first trip to the psych ER at thirteen. Surely bipolar depression was too extreme a rationalization for her fourth trip here? And yet, as she continues to look at the messy scrawl, a certain kind of knowing dawns on her, and all of a sudden, she is swept up in a wave of relief. She asks the doctor which one it is. She has heard that there is more than one kind. The impatient physician returns to the form and scrawls another messy number "1" at the end of the diagnosis.

After the diagnosis of bipolar 1, she remembers a chant from her childhood, a cheer that went something like, "We're number one / not number two / we're going to kick the / s___t out of you!" This makes her laugh whenever she thinks about the difference between bipolar 1 and 2. The diagnosis seems to ignite a feeling of levity in her. Suddenly, something makes sense where before, there were only questions and frustration.

Bipolar 1 explains the paranoia, the mania, the psychotic breaks, and the dissociation she has struggled with for years. It gives words to her feelings and actions. It doesn't cure her, but it gives definition to the amorphous questions she's had about her mental health for sixteen years.

Months before the trip to the psychiatric emergency room at twenty-four, she is sent to the pharmacy to fill out a prescription. When she reaches the window, she sees an older Black woman. Her skin is pale and freckled but it is clear that she is a Black woman. She is stylishly and modestly dressed in a black shirt. She can imagine her at a younger age taking as great care with her appearance as she does now. Her lips and nails are bright red. Glasses sit on her nose framing her eyes with silver rims. The woman looks at her sweaty face standing listlessly behind the counter and says, "I love your dress." This strikes her as an unusual statement. It is an old dress from college designed to look like many brightly colored handkerchiefs sewn together in a random array. But it still looks ok and so she murmurs a quietly found "thank you" to the woman in the window.

The woman behind the counter has no eyebrows, just two thin lines to imitate where they used to be. There are no visible tan lines or shading. You can tell she hasn't had eyebrows for a very long time. Raising the skin on her face where her eyebrows used to be, she looks at her large afro hair through the thick glass of the window. "You know I had a friend who had, you know, very *coarse* hair, just like yours. But when she would perm it, you know, straighten it, it would lie down so pretty. She had hair like yours. I can tell from looking you have that type of hair that, you know, is very *coarse* but would just lie down pretty." She peeks her white teeth out between red-painted lips.

She sees only now that the woman is wearing a black, brittle wig. It is ever so slightly off-kilter and just a bit too waxy to be real. It fans out around her face and high apple cheekbones in wisps, like she has brushed and styled and stored it every night with care since the first day she started wearing it. Because this woman means the words as a compliment, she makes up her mind to take them as one. She is there to fill a prescription for medication that she will be placed on and taken off many times in the years between twenty-four and twenty-nine before being told she will have to take them for the rest of her life. She doesn't know that then and feels a slight shame when the woman confirms the name of her anti-psychotic meds through the thick glass. She wonders if this woman knows what they are for. If the woman does know, she doesn't give any indication of her knowledge and fills the prescription in silence.

When the prescription is filled and she has her monthly supply of the chalky pills they give her at times like these, she leaves, stepping out onto the sidewalk. The glass from the building and the white light bouncing off of the sidewalk in a million different directions combine forces to temporarily blind her, and for the first time in many weeks, her eyes begin to well with water.

She is standing on the sidewalk in front of the emergency room doors. And she is smiling. Well, she is standing on the sidewalk in front of the emergency room doors and the edges of her mouth are moving and creeping. Perhaps up, as people like to say. She touches the back of her wrist against her forehead, offering her fanned-out fingers to protect her eyes against the brightness of the sun's rays. She tucks her chin against her chest and opens up an even more impish smile as the wind whips her handkerchief dress in different directions. She considers not for the first time the complicated webbing of the sidewalk, so much like the streams of blood that used to cover the back of her hand. She looks at the doors of the ER, not knowing then that she will be back someday. But in that moment she's wearing a simple dress that she likes, and someone complimented her hair, and the breeze feels nice on her legs. So she moves.

Goat Mouth

NOTA BENE:

Below this short addendum is a piece that was written by extracting excerpts from the journals I kept in the months leading up to a psychotic break. The fragments were written and arranged up until the night before I was involuntarily admitted to the hospital for psychiatric evaluation. Although it was my third time in a psych ward, it was my first time being placed on a 72-hour hold. The first two times I entered a ward it was for a single day and later a single night, once when I was thirteen years old and again at age eighteen. I was twenty-four when this was written. Each note that follows was written before my journals and computer were taken (I assume at the instruction of physicians, although I'm not entirely sure) to help lure me out of my dissociated state. I've added punctuation and line spacing for clarity. But all of the dates, times, and places are exactingly correct, a function of my obsessions with time and timekeeping and time-wasting and mania.

It is scattered, like my thoughts were at that time. It is partial and incomplete and feverish. It is fragmented, like the onset of sickness usually is. At first, illness comes in little pieces (an errant cough, an unusual tiredness, an odd behavior) and then it suddenly drops on you like a cresting wave. At least that's how it was for me. My writing was caught up in that sickness, both a cause and a manifestation of the disease in my mind. It got sucked under that wave with the rest of my body, denying me air or room or separation. I had a psychology professor in college who told us that the most important function of the human brain was to determine what was "me" and "not me." It's what prevents us from touching a table and assuming that the table and our hands are now the same thing. When I wrote this, I lost track of what was "me" and "not me." It was like looking far out at the ocean and not being able to tell which blue was the water and which blue was the sky.

And I was so afraid. But I want to tell you the truth.

* * *

(Started) October 9th, 2014 8:25 PM

I am a Guerilla Girl writer. I was out here trying to guerilla girl write. Can I preach? Sometimes there is harmony in the breakdown.

Summer 2013

UNC Chapel Hill, North Carolina. In search of Millie-Christine McKoy, (Un)Famed African-American twins born into slavery in 1851. Born in the self same state if not in the self same spot. Toured the world as a musical singing duet, medical sideshow exhibition, American freak show. Attached by their conjoined vagina until their death in 1912.

Posted on Instagram.

"Recreation of the Hayes Plantation library."

{I am standing on the brink of where it was most dangerous for a slave to go.}

"This life sized bronze statue of Sir Walter Raleigh scared the shit out of me when I turned around."

"Dunce" and **"Dark"**: spoken, not dictated. Strangers. Early childhood.

01/06/2014

6:26 PM

Be not my pen a prophecy gild guided like my tongue

Sunday July 13th 2014

1:36 PM

Place: sitting on an overpriced towel w/ zebra stripes that I bought for far too much money in Miami when I forgot mine at home.

Lawn of Yale College cross campus. I am facing Calhoun College, SML library is on my right. My back is to a tree that blocks my view of WLH. There is shade & wind and a little sunshine.

SWIMMING:

I wanted to mark this moment as the precipice of my ambition. I have been toying with these words for far too long now ("Precipice of ambition") and needed to work them out. I don't know how to explain this, but I am consistently gripped with a profound sense of anxiety about my talents…

I feel an almost overwhelming sense of competence that I have never felt before. I have finally come to accept that a large part of my success in life might actually be inherent.

Tuesday July 15th 2014

at 11:06 PM

The past 2 days were mildly turbulent. I think it might be the rain and isolation that is effecting/affecting (Nota Bene: spelling?) my mood.

Washington Heights
Saturday July 19th 2014

Me and my sister have both grown beautiful together.

Walking tonight through the streets of Manhattan, hand in hand, fingers intertwined, we are lockstep on the sidewalk.

People, especially men, stop to watch us pass, taking up space. We are red-lipped and wide hipped and brightly dressed.

Linking up after all these years, finally friends.

Tuesday July 29th, 2014
1:34 PM

Working in a café today trying to finish something like a completed draft of "I could only say thank you."

I feel unexpectedly tender, although when my sentimentality is at its peak might be the best time to do this.

Finished 1:47 PM

Facebook June 15th 2014

Dad: the man who taught me that before you master the extraordinary you must first become adept at the everyday. That you can't use a short cut unless you understand why the long way works. That there is a difference between quiet and contemplative, bossy and a boss. That standing tall isn't about height (Although I enjoyed watching parades from your shoulders.) That everyday we must strive to do the right thing, whatever that may be. Gifter of my first Patwah/Patois dictionary and Louise Bennett poetry book. Artful weaver of Anansi tales. The man behind the camera of one million childhood photos. Off key singer of Bob Marley, Al Green, and Harry Belafonte. Safe keeper of my first library card and payer of many overdue book fines. Nurturer of inquisitive children and expert healer of the most vulnerable humans. Maker of early morning pancakes, amateur acting/forensics/conference presentation coach, my first museum tour guide, inspirational educator, disco dancing champion, leader of the family cheer team, and (dare I say) friend. An original renaissance soul man. Happy happy happy Daddy's Day. It's been the privilege of a lifetime to be your daughter. All love always

DANIELLE BAINBRIDGE

CELLPHONE WRITINGS:

How it feels to write well

In his essay on sex Wallace Shawn describes writerly inspiration as a small voice whispering and beckoning outside of a distant window. The voice leads the writer to greater depths of understanding and truth.

I find this to be untrue. I have often heard that the reason people hate the sound of their own recorded voice is because to them their voices sound entirely different. Something about the way sound travels through our throats and heads back out to our ear makes this sound, the sound of our own voice, that which resonates both internally and externally, sound unique to us above all others. When it's echoed back to us on recordings it sounds like us, but also unlike us. Therefore because of this combination of internal and external rumbling, no one in the world hears our voices the way we do.

When I am writing...correction, "when I am writing well" I hear this voice. It speaks clearly and assertively in a tone and timbre only I can recognize. It speaks to me loudly as if it were shouting to me from across a shallow room. We are not looking at each other, just listening intensely. And I understand everything it wants to explain. I understand it in its entirety.

Live simply so that others may live

"You should have it all"

That's what they say to me. Because I am:

24

Young in years but

Old in experience

Wise

Pretty (?)

Funny

Woman

A good lover

A giver of good love

A cook

A writer

Owner of a frequently complimented sunshiny type of smile.

A Yale PhD student (take that for what it's worth)

I don't know if I've ever truly accepted all of these various monikers and descriptors. At least I've never assumed them all to be true at the same time. So when people exclaim about "having it all" I always marvel that they presume I am so deserving. "All" usually looks like:

Fame

Recognition

A husband who is taller than me, smarter than me, and makes more money than me

A good job

(Successful) kids

Suburban small town

Fancy electronics

A car that has more seats than butts and a house with more bedrooms than bodies, with perhaps one to spare for guests

I do not want most of the things on this list. I do not want it all, whatever that may mean. I wonder how radically different the world would look if we taught the most powerful amongst us that we don't "deserve it all" but rather that each one of us deserves enough?

Enough looks like:

Clean water and air and food

Sudden smiles

Moonshine fantasies

Free hearts

Healing

Shelter

Good love

Something to shelter. Something we are responsible for housing whether it be a dream, an idea, a memory of the summer rain, or a child.

Something to belong to.

Happiness, purpose, and grace.

Peace, serenity, clarity.

Openness.

Miles to travel and rivers to cross.

That is it I suppose. I will teach this lesson, especially to my daughters and especially to my sons:

You are enough. You deserve enough, even if you have the power to have it all. Give graciously, taking extra time to give praise and thanks to those who have helped you. Love always in the present tense. Do not be afraid.

Good names for daughters

History (my choice)

Hero (history and hero would be great twin names)

Brave (stole this one and hero from cree summers)

Novel (my choice)

Idea (alternative to Isaiah for a boy or boyish girl?)

Clarity

Poetry

Some other thoughts:

Destiny

Serenity

Patience

Judge (to be my namesake, since my name means God is my judge)

Utopia

Manifest (for a boy. Nickname Manny)

Ones I like the best:

Hero

History

Novel

Clarity

Judge

Idea

Poetry

Author (for a boyish girl)

Recently there's been a girl child weighing heavy on my mind. She is dark skinned and big eyed and bow lipped and fat. I think she'll change the world and she will be my daughter. I have started to write names for her here and am seriously thinking all the time about pregnancy. I know it seems so crazy but I think something inside of me is shifting to make room for her. I feel her always pressing down on me and it fills me with an inexplicable joy. I know I should "wait for the right man" but I've never actually believed that and I don't think that she will wait on him either. I need to find a black male donor though. I'm not sure but I see her brown brown body and know her father is black. What does this all mean? Why am I sitting here naming her?

I have also chosen too many names because, to my deepest terror, I am almost positive it will be twin girls…

Written July 11th 2014 at 12:44 PM

Facebook May 28th 2014

On the death of Dr. Angelou

My heart will have to learn a new language of longing to miss this phenomenal woman. Her words have nourished me through some of the darkest struggles and helped me soar to higher heights.

Rest in Power.

August 1st 2014

Dictated, not typed: "You know you ain't shit when your father has to physically carry you to the bathroom."

August 4th 2014:

Sleeping on bed rest, writing on walls.

Instagram: Day 3 with my constant companion. *Little Brother.*

2014 October

Dictated, not typed: "Don't try to deploy some sort of lazy nigger narrative whereby black and brown bodies have to be compelled up to real work."

Dictated, not typed: "It's about knowing the difference between when you're begging, tabling it, saying no, or raising up."

Dictated, not typed: "These places were not designed with my body in mind."

Dictated, not typed: "Don't come in here beating sticks at me like I'm some lazy nigger."

Dictated, not typed: "There are LAYERS to this shit."

Dictated, not typed: "Don't try to come in here and fix to tell me about my raise up."

August 16th 2014 at 11:53 PM

I am more tempestuous feeling than impeccable outline, although I labor under healthy doses of both.

Rehearsal, Twilight Los Angeles 1992, February 2012

Articulated, Ya girl: "Jay if the script says nigger, just say NIGGER. ER, not GA. HARD R."

Oct 19th 2014 7:10 AM, Facebook

I am more impetuous design than impeccable outline, although I labor under healthy dosages of both.

Revised mom letter bday (10/28/2014)

Not more than a handful of months ago I sat up at the dining room table, ready to bang my head against it as I furiously compiled 3 AM revisions. I felt in my spirit that the paper was bad and that there was nothing I could do to fix it.

In the next room lay Paulette asleep on the couch (but easily within earshot), waiting until everything was completed to go to bed, demonstrating a patience with her daughter that in that moment I could not grant myself. A ritual that began many moons ago in high school somehow made the impossible work feel possible again. I cannot number the times I have faltered or stumbled and looked over only to see my mother there, waiting calmly and confidently for me, cheering me on even when no one else was there to watch. I have seen her feet clear the floor with joy for her children, seen her shoulders stoop to bear our loads.

I remember sitting at your feet in the bookstore, my arms wrapped tight around your legs. You were always eager to let your small daughter, the skylark obsessed with gazing, try her hands at the mysteries of wonder. Thank you for allowing me to fly away to far off places in my mind while you remained nearby, content to grant your girl the complexity to get completely carried away with dreaming. Thank you for (too much) hot food, and for being a giver of good love. Thank you for the quotidian, for my black polite tongue and for my P's and Q's manners. For my need to stand up straight so people will know I don't "come from nowhere." Thank you for making sure I come from somewhere. Even though to this day I cannot iron a shirt to meet your exacting specifications, thank you for helping me to savor life's sweets with the spoilage. Thank you for my many alternative educations. Thank you for those first political rallies, for raising us in the Black Law Students Association, for showing me what it means to labor in love, for taking me to vote for the first time when I was 9 years old (and for letting me pull the lever so I would know what it feels like, in part, to change the world). For your fearsome intellect and caring strength. Thank you for our "mommy dates." For believing in me, always, more than I believe in myself. You are mighty. The tough talk soft touch safe haven.

You are always on call. And anything in life I ever got or hoped to get: I got it from my mama.

All love, today, everyday, and always.

Transcribed from cellphone, October 9th 2014

Time stamp 10/06/2014 4:42 PM

Goat Mouth: The piece about my friends who are survivors.

Time stamp 10/06/2014 5:13 PM

Started wearing a watch again for the first time this summer.

Time stamp 10/08/2014

Goat mouth: A story about me, my mom, my sister, aunts and grandmothers all being survivors.

Time stamp 10/08/2014 2:44 PM

Goat mouth: Jamaican Patwah word for being able to prophesize. Always Negative.

My mother, my sister, and I are finally growing beautiful. Together. 3 force ripe, false ripe, but still (im)perfect creatures operating in unison and synchronizing our steps.

2014 October

For Tyler Kaneesha and Ryan. The Allies. For all The Allies.

October {2014}

Dictated, not typed: *"My mother comes from a place so remote we got out of the car last time we went because the engine was dragging on the floor."*

Dictated, not typed: *"don't tell me how to organize black people."*

Dictated, not typed: *"If your rhetoric don't match your footwork, then fuck it, you're not my ally! How the fuck you gunna approach me like I wasn't raised Black Church?"*

Dictated, not typed: *"I have accurate memories stretching back to age 2 or 3, which may be contributing to my summer's hyper-mania. I understand rules and that's how I sat for a week and taught myself to translate a little French. I have a little Latin, a Little Spanish, a (very) Little Italian, and now a Little French. But my first language is Patwah, which helps me combine them all. Likkle but tallawah."*

Dictated, not typed: *"Sometimes an artist that is bored is just looking for a physical praxis."*

Facebook, September 2014: #Fbf to one of my earliest publication efforts, "Virtual comfort in Any Season" by Mrs. Bouchard's 5th grade class. Things of note include:

1) my serious scowl

2) my half pony pigtails

3) those army green cargo pants I wore at least once a week for a year.

4) I refer to my family as migrating geese in this story. #Diaspora

5) I've always written about the Caribbean.

6) My parents saved this for 13 years.

7) My bios always said "Danielle wants to grow up to be a poet and a doctor." Back then I meant physician

October 2014

Dictated, not typed: *"I was always scared after I dropped pre-med that being a full time writer was a lazy choice."*

Dictated, not typed: *"These bitches out here think they can run me like I'm step and fucking fetch it."*

March 2012, Intro to Acting

I am cast in the two-woman show A Couple of White Chicks Sitting Around Talking. Words escape. Me.

August 2013

Dictated, not typed: *"Sometimes I have to burn or hide my writing if it's something I can never tell. I stick the words in secret places: the mattress, my underwear drawer, under the couch, and then allow myself to be surprised when I find them later. Don't you have things like that too? Things you can never tell?"*

August 2014

Meditated, not typed: *It's like I'm out here triggering like crazy Mommy.*

September 2014

Articulated for the first time out loud: *I need to find a way to speak my piece and keep my peace.*

August 08/14/2014 12:14 AM

Today I received so much love. I am in wonder. I feel more confident than I ever have. I want to publish a book. I have looked better and felt better every year but now I'm finally able to look back on my sullen chubby black girl silence and smile. I was so round faced and innocent and sweet. Maybe I felt like an ugly child. We are made to think so little of ourselves as children.

But my eyes were round and bright. My smile was keen and intelligent. I was smart and chubby and healthy. What is so wrong with that? I was beloved by family and friends and teased by few. I was mostly covered and protected by close ties to relatives and friends alike.

So now I am beautiful in my own way. Full and radiant with it, and I am content to be still in the eye of storms of unaccustomed attention. But I am still, silent, and secretly beaming, shielding myself from their glares. I am content to be myself and let it be. (Finished 12:22 AM)

October 2014

Ya girl articulating: *Sometimes I find it embarrassing how hard I have to work. I mean, it's just never taken me that long to get stuff done.*

Gwendolyn Brooks: *"Everybody here is infirm"*

C.L.R. James, Black Jacobins: *"Refinements of cruelty."*

Dictated not typed October 2014: *"My empathy response just seemed really low, ya know?"*

Articulated, too many times to count: *"Being raised by two medical clinicians makes me feel like a damn lab rat sometimes."*

Articulated 10/07/2014: *"I notice that sometimes I tick or twitch in counts of 2 and 4 and 8. Like music."*

I started singing again.

Articulated, my father: *"You're a little oppositional defiant. But so are most good leaders."*

Ya girl articulating: *"When I fell back into my black girl silence, my writing started S-C-R-E-A-M-I-N-G. I fell down on my writing. Threw my whole body on it."*

12/17/2014 8:50 AM

May/Be

Hallucination: that which only the witness can witness.

Fever Dream: that which only the witness may witness.

Fantasy: that which only the witness can allow you to witness.

Nightmare: everything that we must witness, alone.

**10/09/2014
7:06 PM**

<u>Goat Mouth:</u>

English translation: <u>Jinx</u>[123]

---

[1] Named for John C. Calhoun, graduate of Yale College and supporter of slavery.

[2] Warriors. People who have seen some shit and come through the other side.

[3] Literal translation.

Cyar

Cuh-yar: Accent on "yar." Jamaican Patwah/Patois for Car.

I knew intimately the method of its destruction, though I had never seen it burning.

* * *

September 11th, 2001, in the New York City suburb of New Rochelle, NY. I am starting the first week of 6th grade in a new all-girls' Catholic school. I am short, very chubby, and very brown, unlike the majority of my classmates. A nun in my new school once told us, "The only difference between a girl who chews gum and a grazing cow is the look of intelligence on the face of the cow." On this morning we are chattering and chirping before falling silent as the overhead speakers crackle to life. First we pray, then we pledge, then we listen for announcements. Swinging my fat legs underneath the starched hem of my freshly pleated skirt, I gaze longingly at the clock. I do not remember now what time it was then, only that I desperately wished the hands would move faster and free me from the boredom of my first period history class.

The overhead speaker crackles back to life and we hear our principal's stoic voice. She is the same nun who said the line about the grazing cows.

Second announcement of the day: "There's been an accident in New York City."

Third announcement of the day: "Can the following girls please come down to the office?" followed by a list of random names.

Fourth announcement of the day: We are all going home.

I did not see my parents again until much later that night. My mother squeezes her body onto a train still willing to leave Manhattan for Westchester County. My father returns even later than her from his hospital in the Bronx. He lies on his back in his bedroom watching the news, staying separate from the rest of our family. I creep into his room and silently perch on the edge of the bed. At that age I was fascinated by the forbidden world of adults. I loved to linger in the kitchen and hear the stories about the men that my aunties and mother would share. I wanted to press myself through the thick smoke that hovered above the heads of my uncles and fake uncles in my godmother's basement, to taste the strong rum and weak beer the men drank beside the bar. I craved to know the secrets that grown bodies knew. So, this moment sitting next to my father and his rarely shown sadness holds me transfixed. I savor the silence, trying not to breathe too hard lest he remembers that I am there. We sit in silence watching the now infamous images of the planes moving into and back out of the Twin Towers on repeat, as the stunned TV broadcasters fast-forward and rewind the tapes again and again.

My father and I finish the first news hour in silence. The footage loops back to repeat itself. Finding the courage to speak, I say, "Why are we still watching this?" My shoulders curve in towards my stomach and my back aches from sitting still. I remember a faint fear mixed with a creeping boredom.

He tells me that this moment will change the rest of my life and so we have to watch it. I do not think of 9/11 as the urtext of my understanding of world politics. I don't even recall it as the moment I recognized what violence is. It was an hour spent perched on the edge of my parents' bed, watching something that I didn't comprehend. It was being eleven, impatient to grow up, and confused. It was hearing the hushed voices of adults whispering in anxiety and anger. I felt older being allowed to sit there and watch that. I observed panicked, bloodied faces scrambling through the rubble, and hands grasping desperately at other dusty hands or empty air.

In the years that followed, my father would tell me that he came home late that night because the city, in a panic, had told all first responders to stand by. So, he and the other physicians in his hospital in the Bronx hurried to discharge non-critical patients so that they could prepare every bed possible for the incoming flow of injured victims. It wasn't until hours of waiting had passed that they realized no patients would come. They had almost all died.

This is my first memory of seeing death, of feeling intimately acquainted with dying. I went to bed that night and wondered how everything would change.

* * *

Ten years later I am standing on the periphery of my paternal great-grandfather's land in Saint Andrew, Jamaica. Christmastime 2011. He was the father of my paternal grandmother. Dead long before I was born, I knew of him only through my father's stories, and only then in passing as "Mass Cay" (shorthand for Caleb). Not too far from my mother's familial homestead, this plot of land represents the final country outpost of my Kingston, Jamaica relatives. My father and his brother spent their summers here, alternating between work and mischief. We return here once every few years on our pilgrimages to Jamaica, telling stories and watching over the graves of my great-grandfather and great-grandmother. At the time of this 2011 visit, Miss Cynthia (my great-grandfather's last common-law wife before his death) is the official owner of the land, watched over by my great-uncle Herbie. Although he is technically my father's uncle, he functions more like my father's brother since he was born to Mass Cay late in life and is only a few years older.

When we arrive that day we find Miss Cynthia, family historian, lover of children, masterful cook in her little outdoor kitchen, in the final throes of debilitating dementia. Her strong feet are swollen to the size of cooked hams, her dress in tatters and soaked with urine. I look at her face, the woman who watched my siblings and I scatter across her front yard with glee, who had cooked me good food, who remembered the years all of the children were born, who taught me not to be afraid of the outhouse when I was a child (but nevertheless placed a bucket outside when I refused to pee in the darkened room), who fed me until I was fat and kissed me with her one-toothed mouth, who always took care to overfeed us and tell us we were "nice." That woman sits there numb, sometimes mumbling absently to herself. In a fleeting moment of clarity, she recognizes my mother, asking her when she gained so much weight, in the usual brisk manner of elderly Jamaicans. She asks my father the same question. I realized then that she remembers nothing past my parents' wedding in 1987. I was born in 1990. It was as if I never existed. Years later I will go through this same painful process of forgetting with my maternal grandfather, reminding me that people have called dementia "the long goodbye." With each memory that slips away from my elders, I feel the edges of my reality shift, for who am I if I'm not the object and subject of their love and loving memories? On that day in 2011, I resigned myself to silence, listening to her softly babbling until it was time to take our leave and go to the hotel.

My Uncle Herbie leads us through the thickets and every once in a while, I stop to take photographs. Of the trees, of my brother walking through the canopy of the sugar cane, of my mother ruefully contemplating the landscape that raised her, of my father laughing at the brown spotted cows grazing on the hillside. My mother is sure-footed, even while wearing white flip-flops, and teases me about my clumsiness in the hilly terrain. She reminds me that she is, after all, a country girl at heart. I take pictures of myself scrambling up rock faces and tripping through tall grass and shuffling past the places where

Mass Cay and the first of his children's mothers are buried. I take pictures of these graves but not of the car wreck.

I do not think it is wise, although I spend many minutes lingering here and creating a memory from heart. I am fearful that a picture will trap this thing to me and will make us indelibly tied. I do not want to go back through my vacation photos later and have to explain this to the others. I don't want to explain why I took a picture of something so unrelated to me and so grotesque. But I want to remember, even though I am unsure of what I am seeing. So I write it down.

When we reached the car, it was entirely by accident. Herbie points to it and explains that a murder had taken place here several years ago. The community believed that the men in the car were first forced to crash, and then set on fire as an act of political retaliation. I do not know these men's names or whether the story is true. My uncle is known in the family as one who isn't wonderful with detailed retellings. A quick search online reveals dozens of similar stories. The words "murder, Jamaica, politics, car crash" yield a seemingly endless stream of stories and faces, not all of them dead. I only know that the car stood there, blackened and hollowed like a burnt shell, clinging so precariously to the ledge that it seemed apparent to me that the murderers thought whoever was inside was surely not meant to live at all, let alone to survive such a tragedy. How can a body suffer so?

I pull up short beside the driver's side door. My father cautions me to stay back, my feet still unsteady in my Converse sneakers on the sloping muddy ridge beside the hard gravel road. My legs feel coltish and unfamiliar as I look at it. I am not wearing tall work boots like my uncle; my sneakers are woefully inadequate in the rugged landscape. My mother jokes that the shoes have probably never walked across real mud before. Now they are caked with bright red dirt.

I inch closer and closer before I stop. How would we even begin to fix this car? It seems to me that many of the parts have been taken after the crash. I imagine that even charred they must have fetched a small sum of money as scrap metal. I want to touch the car's exterior, but I do not. I have never wanted to die in a struggle. A fire. Drowning. Suffocation. It seems that this car represents the worst of all punishments. I look from my red dirt-covered shoes back to the exterior and imagine I can see the faces of the men inside.

When we leave at nightfall, hoping to avoid dangerous driving conditions back to Montego Bay, my uncle touches my father's hand in a warm handshake. Two men that grew up as boys together, they now live worlds apart: my father in an American suburb and my uncle in the Jamaican countryside. Yet together, in this place, they are like boys again. It seems they are in secret agreement. They whisper hushed words not meant for Miss Cynthia's ears, as I am sure they have done many times in the past. They are likely talking about what medications she needs and her end-of-life care. When we load into the car my uncle stands back from the wheels of the vehicle to wave at us. Rapping twice on my mother's passenger side window he tells us to be careful on the road, that it's election time. With that, we wave and depart.

The trip down the mountain road that will take us back to the main roads snaking their way to Kingston or the North

Shore of the island is one I have always hated. Barely wide
enough for one car to pass, the road is wrapped around the
outer extremities of the mountain. Snaking its way precariously
to the top, every year the road suffers more and more erosion
from all of the human traffic (both bodily and vehicular) and
the rainy climate. Once it has become too narrow for vehicles,
the road is carved further into the mountain's surface to extend
its width. Flying around blind corner after blind corner with
only the blaring sound of a car horn to alert you to approaching
drivers (that is if they remember to use their lights and horn at
all), as a child I was always convinced that I would die on this
road to my great-grandparents' house.

It seemed to me immaterial whether my demise would
be en route to Mass Cay's grave or to Miss Cynthia's outdoor
kitchen. But my cowardice around heights and my own innate
sense of hyperbole couldn't disconnect these hairpin turns and
narrow shoulders from the billboards on Kingston highways
announcing greater traffic regulations. Every year hundreds lose
their lives in automobile accidents in Jamaica. The same is true
of the US. Dying felt somehow closer on this narrow ledge,
looking down into the endless expanse of thick, wooded lands
imprinted with my parents' childhood feet. It is on the shoulder
of this road, the road where I always imagined I would die as
a child, that the burned-out car remained stuck. Below it lay
a seemingly endless expanse of vegetation, waiting for a strong
wind to rock the car's carcass over the ledge and bury it from
sight. I still wonder why that car had no smell. In Manhattan
my mother described the smell of the bodies from the Twin
Towers as one of the worst things she's ever encountered. For
years the car remained there, nestled into the rock face, its
metal parts disintegrating before making room for the unruly

vegetation peeking up through its hollow frame. It seemed nothing but the tangle of stunted shoots and flowers was keeping it fixed to the rocky face of the road.

An acting coach once told me that to walk with poise I should imagine a string tied to the top of my head with an invisible man at the top gently pulling me upwards. I remember at that moment on the roadside it felt as if the strings had gone slack, leaving me splay legged and buckled on the side of the road. Something had shifted beneath me and the present slipped in. I was surrounded on all sides by the reality of my life, which until that moment had existed in my mind as an endless spool of undeveloped film. It was suddenly unraveled and all that I saw were the repeating images I had already known: the tire swing in my neighbor's yard I'd always eyed with envious greed, the pink-tipped white magnolias turning downwards as they drifted into the green grass of our lawn, that same lawn rushing up to meet my face the many times I fell from the magnolia tree's higher branches, the blue benches at the park with the loose boards that I would jam my fingers into until they got stuck. And now a car: possibly blue, definitely destroyed. Faces I have never seen trapped inside (I imagine what they looked like.) My pristine white sneakers rimmed with an outline of reddish mud, politely pressed together. All there, all connected, all present, all pressing. I have seen those images more than some of my beloved family photos.

My uncle's rapt gaze as he inspected the outside of the car, his stillness, and his silence were meant as an instruction: these images, this version of the present, will change your life. And so, you have to watch. You have to witness. And I did. That day I learned to alert my senses to a new way of seeing and understanding. That day I stood rapt in the gaze of violent action and somehow, I felt that I saw it and it saw me. It was then that I realized my father's intentions in 2001 and my uncle's intentions in 2011. They were giving me the last tangible thing they had, in the face of distress, in the face of uncertainty and trauma. I was tied to my peers now. My peers were not only the ones who were my age when they saw images of fallen towers, but also the ones who were my age when they remembered days like this one at the side of the road.

We all bear witness.

We all witness different things.

When I was in high school, I was shocked to learn that despite driving for decades in Jamaica my maternal grandfather has never had a driver's license. When I ask him about this shocking revelation he responds with his usual quick wit: "Remember, my granddaughter, license can't drive cyar."

Be careful on the road, it's election time.

* * *

January 2015. Days after Christmas, two months after my third psych emergency room visit, four months after I have had major surgery on my right ovary. The morning is cold and unassuming. My father and I are driving in the car. This is an unremarkable morning activity. I have taken countless car rides in the morning with my dad. Everyone in my family has. Over the years he has driven our family all over the United States and North America: three 24-hour stints to Florida, a disastrous "vacation" to Cincinnati, Ohio, innumerable trips over the hump of New York into Canada, day trips to Hershey, Pennsylvania to see the chocolate factory. Of all the members of my family, my dad is the one who loves to drive the most. He taught all three of his children to drive with a stern but guiding hand.

Once when I had just gotten my learner's permit, I pulled into our uphill driveway a little too fast and almost crashed into the garage door. On instinct my father threw my mother's old Honda into park, bringing us to an abrupt halt. My little brother laughed gleefully from the back seat as I ran to my room in embarrassment. Hours later, my father gave his signature knock on my closed bedroom door: one long knock, followed by four short, and two long. He coaxed me back into the car, demanding I drive once more around the block. Afterwards he told me he wanted me to remember that I was more than one mistake.

On this day in early 2015 I am twenty-four and still healing from the turmoil of the previous months. Two hospitalizations (separately for my body and my mind) have left me shaken and unsteady. But I am chatting rapidly with my father, and he is listening with patient care. This is a part of our routine: I talk, he listens and provides occasional advice. We are on our way to one of my childhood best friend's condo because my friend, her mother, and I are going to watch her try on wedding dresses for her upcoming nuptials. I desperately wish now that I could remember what we were talking about then, but the ordinariness of the day and the conversation has wiped my memory blank of detail. All I remember now is the moment I realized something was wrong.

As we enter the parking lot of the condo complex, the same complex my friend and her mother have lived in since we were in middle school, we approach three speed bumps. I know these bumps well from my father's high school driving lessons, since he'd often let me practice by driving to my friend's house. My father, a creature of habit and discipline, always told me to tap the brakes as we approached the higher-than-average bumps to ensure that the car didn't bounce too high. But today we hit the first bump at full speed and go flying over it, landing back on the blacktop with a dull thud. I say to him without turning, "You didn't slow down?" I say it like a question because it doesn't make sense. I turn to my dad and for the first time on our drive, I notice that the left side of his body is paralyzed. His eyes are distant and unfocused, his eyelids blinking rapidly as his limp, but still mobile right wrist attempts to steer the wheel. His spine is snapped straight, almost bowing backward towards the seat and his usually intelligent face is slack.

I could set my watch by my father's regularity. Once in college, I said offhandedly to an older Black woman that I wasn't sure where my father was. Mistaking my statement for abandonment, she sympathetically laid her hand on mine and asked me where he could be. Confused, I glanced up at the clock, noted the time, and said he must be on his way to pick up my mother from work. That's how deeply I have learned his habits. His stability and regularity were the backbone of my childhood. So, when I see this contorted zombie in the driver's seat instead of my father I panic. Something is wrong.

Dad would never:

1) Go sailing over speed bumps

2) Drive recklessly

3) Stop listening to my endless stories

4) Endanger the lives of any of his children or wife or family

We are rolling downhill in the parking lot now and picking up speed. We go flying over two more speed bumps before we exit the lot and careen out into the street. We are speeding through back roads that are as familiar to me as the back of my hand, images of trees and houses zipping by my window in a blur. My father's one hand is struggling to hold on to the wheel, fighting against the paralyzing shudders that are wracking his body. Even though his mind is distant and far away, it's as if some instinct is fighting through the fog so he can steer the car and save our lives.

I am screaming: his name, the word "Dad," curse words, and incoherent pleas to an unseen force for the car to slow down. We continue speeding through the back streets directly outside the parking lot, crossing two blessedly empty intersections before he passes out, going limp behind the wheel. In my frenzy and fear I assume that my father is dead. I assume he is dead behind the wheel of a still speeding car, his foot glued to the gas, and that I too will die soon if we do not slow down.

After the second intersection, we hop the curb in front of some stranger's house and drive up into their lawn. The tires of our car are shredding their suburban grass as we quickly approach a massive tree at a speed that will surely kill or at least injure us both. As the tree looms closer, I remember the day in the car when I almost hit the garage door. My mind empties, preparing for impact and death and in my last rational moment I pull up the gear and shift the car quickly into park. The car slows down a fraction and we make impact with the tree. The next thing I know we are surrounded by the sound of metal on bark and engine on roots. The airbags explode in our faces, and all I can see is the faint pink color of the insides of my closed eyelids where the sun is shining through. My trembling hand is still gripping the gear, and I accidentally slip it into reverse. Suddenly we are moving again, the car spinning backwards before making a 360-degree turn and settling against another bank of trees at the edge of the lawn.

My body, slick with sweat but still alive, comes back to itself and I turn to my father. This is the person whose love, alongside my mother, has been my anchored place in the world. He lies so still. "He's dead. Daddy's dead," I think to myself, my whole heart broken. My father, who coached me in speech and debate for seven years, and cured me of my childhood shyness. My father, the reason I swore when I was seven years old that I would never change my last name because one day I would be Dr. Bainbridge just like him. My father, whose belief in me has far exceeded my belief in myself at most times in my life. My father, whose quiet demeanor and gentle humor I inherited. My father, the family historian, driver, disciplinarian, and steadfast champion. This is my father, who is dead in the car. His body is still slumped over the wheel, the airbags slowly deflating around us. "Daddy's dead." I think this to myself again, afraid to give breath behind the words, not even embarrassed to be using the more infantilized version of his name. I have not called him that in years, but at this moment I feel small and hopeless. I am scared.

I flex my legs and realize they are still working, somehow miraculously uncrushed by our run-in with the tree. I test my arms and neck and realize that they are also fine. In a daze I continue to test my body, afraid to look back at my father, because if I look then it is real, and if it is real then I will have to face it, and if I have to face it then I am alone in a car with my father's dead body.

After a short but impossibly long time, I reach over the airless airbags to touch his shoulder, expecting to find it cold. I touch him gingerly at first. "Dad?" I whisper his name like a question, as if I am a child and I am afraid to wake him up one of the countless mornings my siblings and I crawled into my parents' bed in the early hours of the weekend.

I touch him one more time. "Daddy?" I say it like I did when I wanted to coax him into making us pancakes early on a Sunday, us three kids singing backup to his off-tune renditions of Motown and "No Woman, No Cry."

"Daddy, please," I say one more time, shaking him briskly. I am ready to bargain with the Devil himself if I can just bring him back to life. I shake his shoulder in my hand and feel the January cold creeping into the car and through my jacket. I remember the time in college when I took a cheap bus from Philadelphia into Manhattan, and he came to pick me up. I had dressed inappropriately for the weather and by the time he arrived I was shaking on the side of the road in Chinatown. Embarrassed about my lack of preparedness I didn't say anything, choosing instead to sit on my hands for warmth. Silently my father crossed over three lanes of Manhattan rush hour traffic, ignoring blaring horns and angry glares, before pulling over. He hopped out of the car and took his coat off, giving it to me in unceremonious silence. I burrowed down into its familiar brown sleeves, forgetting to even say so much as thank you. I heard once that the sign of a good childhood is when you aren't made to feel responsible for the feelings and lives of the adults around you. In many ways I had a childhood like this, where I failed to comprehend that my parents had any other interests outside of me and my two siblings. They didn't even take a vacation without us until we were all in our twenties. This stability was shattered like the front end of our car, the metal wrapped around the trunk of a tree along with my former sense of safety.

In our totaled car I give up on speaking and decide to shake him one last time. One last time to try before I get out and find help.

And then all of a sudden, his eyes are open. He wakes up like Lazarus in the Bible, the one man in the scripture who supposedly cheated death.

My mouth hangs open. "He's alive?" I think to myself, too scared and superstitious to even utter the words, afraid that I will call bad fate back to us inside the car. As we both stumble out of the wreck on unsteady legs his speech is mixed up and his usually articulate sentences jumbled (Something we will later learn is another effect of the disease.) He is dazed, not remembering what happened.

In the weeks that follow the accident I become convinced that I was born under a dark and unlucky star, slipping further into the throws of my still-undiagnosed bipolar depression.

"First surgery, then the psych ward, then this? Surely this isn't normal?" I think to myself. A trifecta of sadness.

My father tells me later that me being in the car saved his life. I don't believe him because lifesavers aren't born under unlucky dark stars. Lifesavers do not contemplate suicide when so many people in their family want desperately to live and live longer and live well. I don't truly believe that I saved anyone, until a father of my friend tells me the same thing many years later. Even now the thought of driving causes cold sweat and shallow breaths. It shames me that a task that most people think of as mundane has morphed into one of my greatest fears.

Even so it is six-and-a-half years before I will drive a car again. Six-and-a-half years before I shift a car out of park and into gear and drive slowly on the road.

* * *

How do I reconcile the watchful daughter, the curious witness, and the grateful survivor? How do I go home if I must always be careful on the road?

I Could Only Say Thank You
(Part 2)

Let me stop here to say a few (or many) words about my roommate (_____). She was a tallish, almost reflectively pale white woman with a large chest and small frame glasses. Her long blonde hair tapered to an end around the center of her back, and she frequently pinned it to the crown of her head with an array of skinny, clean-tipped paintbrushes. Upon first meeting me she tucked her chin in towards her chest and offered me a small half-smile, her sharp short canine teeth inching over her lower lip in a look that I came to associate with her happiness. The sum of these facts in combination with her self-professed love of all things comic book/sci-fi/fantasy related (and her insistence on naming them as deliberately separate spheres of interest) always gave her a strangely elfish air, as if she was thinking of something secretly funny and mischievous.

After a brisk handshake, she said to me, "You must be my roommate from Yale." The first time she mentioned it, she said the final word almost entirely neutrally. She was merely stating facts: she had heard where I came from and was repeating it now to break the ice. Later, when she knew me better, she tended to say the word Yale with a hint of theatricality as if mocking a fairytale far-off place. This made me like her immediately. I had already decided to neither hide nor over-emphasize the name of my home institution in a reflexive desire to be perceived as likable. I have often seen a sudden change of expression when I say this word. The weary eye squint, the raised eyebrow of unfeigned surprise, the anger, the snide remarks, the overly curious fascination. I did not want to lead with this identifier. I would later come to cherish (_____)'s almost complete indifference to my race and my school and my social class and my afro as the most valuable marker of her friendship. She just spoke. To me. She also became the fiercest protector of my secrets while abroad, a job she took just as seriously as glaring at the men who tried (or succeeded) in touching my hair. As a result, she is the only person I'm still in constant contact with to this day.

At the table in front of the restaurant that first day I arrived, she explained to me that what we both thought would be an independent living situation with our own rooms and kitchen access would actually be a shared attic bedroom in a house boasting three generations of very interdependent Italian women. "They're nice. It's *way* better than the place they had me staying the first night. After that, I had to sleep on the couch in the boys' apartment until they got me a new room." She laughed all of a sudden as if this were a joke and so I laughed with her. It took me a few days of drinking cheap wine and playing cards in the disarray of the aforementioned "boys" apartment before I realized why this might be funny. After we finished eating at the table, she grabbed the handle of my suitcase without any preamble and guided me to the theatre doors. I admired her moxie and assertiveness and so I followed along in silence.

The theatre, like everything at Yale, was designed to look much older than it actually is. The rumor was that the theatre had been renovated sometime during the 20th-century. However, it seemed to me that the town (not being extremely wealthy) never quite captured the magic of what I assumed was the building's former glory. Instead, they opted for a strange hodgepodge of architectural elements: Grecian pillars stood next to red velvet box seats lifted straight out of late 19th-century Paris. Everything was overwhelmingly red, from the chairs, to the walls, to the accents near the entrance.

Someone had been commissioned to create a Sistine Chapel-esque ceiling mural, but the inconsistencies in the various elements and artistry made it seem as if many hands had tested their craft against this painting at different points in time. I noticed on this first day that some of the fat cherubs and naked ladies have uneven nipples, while some are missing nipples entirely. Another figure looks faintly cross-eyed. I pointed this out quietly to (_____), who boldly stated that all the Italian women she had ever known had very pale nipples that almost matched the color of their olive skin. She then went on to describe what she feels are the ethnic and racial differences in the various areolae she's encountered. I asked why she had seen so many women's nipples since I knew she was engaged to a man who had recently returned home to New Jersey after a weeklong Italian vacation to help her settle in before the show. She shrugged nonchalantly. As a costume and fashion design student, she'd seen her fair share of naked ladies, mostly models. As a survivor of seven years of all-girls Catholic education, so have I. During particularly rough rehearsals or late-night cramming sessions, I tipped my head back against the soft headrests, sat in the center seat of the middle aisle, and stared up at the lopsided nips.

We placed my overly large luggage in the wings of the stage before we emerged back into the heat-soaked cobblestones of the street, cigarettes in hand. "These are the smokers," she told me baldly, pointing around at the people congregating in a circle at the mouth of the entrance. She passes me her lighter and I forget about the promises I made to myself on the plane to quit before I reached Italy, to give it up for the summer in an attempt to stem the habit I had developed during college. But in that moment, I silenced those doubts and accepted what she was offering, lifting my head up from where it was buried in my overstuffed backpack frantically searching for a lighter I'd stored somewhere within its cavernous confines in what felt like three days ago in New York.

I inhaled hard on my cigarette and passed the lighter back to (_____). Later that day after rehearsal she dragged me and my bags through the main arteries of town to where we were staying. On the way there she showed me the highlights: supermarket, cigarette store (There are entire stores here for tobacco, like our liquor stores, which seems to be a strange concept in a town where you can buy most alcohol with your groceries.), cafés, restaurants, and finally home. We arrived at the locked gates of a four-story beautiful light-stucco historic building. The inside had been converted into two-story apartments. The tenants coming downstairs watched as we struggled to lift my bag up four flights, trailing at the coattails of our hostess who seemed to be moving impossibly fast for a woman in four-inch platform heels. (_____) and I were winded but already giggling like girlhood friends.

When we reached the top of the stairs, puffing like dehydrated animals, our hostess pointed us onwards to a narrow winding metal staircase. It was beautifully crafted with flat gleaming wood slats for steps. We were careful not to let my luggage scrape the steps or the walls, and finally reached the home we ended up sharing for almost five weeks. Our hostess explained that this used to be her daughter's childhood bedroom, pointing to where that same daughter sat studying medical textbooks and smoking cigarettes at her desk.

The room was small and narrow but impeccably clean. Everything within it looked exceptionally girly, even though there wasn't a single hint of pink in sight. All of the furniture was the same gleaming white as the walls, with several built-in bookcases and a neat little desk completing the image. Our clean-conscious hostess asked us not to cook in her kitchen, although she was happy to feed us and have us store light snacks in the refrigerator. In my first week in the apartment, I saw the adult daughter walking around naked at 2 a.m. By my third, the grandmother saw me naked as I raced across the hall from the bathroom to my bedroom right before dawn (I assumed they had all left for the weekend and was wrong). By the fourth week, I completely forgot to care.

I have never been a person particularly inclined towards roommates. But (_____) seemed predestined to change my mind. Sleeping on our side-by-side twin beds every night we soon unconsciously matched our schedules to get up for rehearsals at the same time. On my second night in Italy, I unearthed my stockpile of American junk food and we both discovered a mutual love for the kinds of shitty treats you can only get in tubes (Pringles, Oreos, trail mix with more chocolate than protein, king-size bags of Skittles). Lying out on the rug we ate our way giddily through our contraband picnic, carefully hiding the wrappers at the bottom of our little trash can because we weren't allowed to eat in our room. Soon we decided to share groceries. With the exception of our tastes in cheeses (I became enamored with Italian gorgonzola while she remained steadfastly faithful to Swiss.) we were living almost the same life, experience for experience, every day. The sleep, the food, the travel, the weekend trips to nearby cities in our hostess' car, the Italian brand of menthols we both began smoking to replace our preferred American brands. Our synchronization was entirely unplanned and yet seemed oddly natural.

I told her about my life, and she understood. We talked about psychiatrists and therapists and depression and experimenting with drugs and sex and *The Golden Girls*. We talked like we had been talking forever, and it felt that way up in our little attic bedroom with the gleaming white walls. One day, we used a broomstick to swat down a hornet's nest that was stuck up in the rafters of our room. When it hit the ground, we were terrified to find at least a dozen petrified spiders on the inside. We swept them all onto a plate and flushed them swiftly down the toilet. It became one of our favorite stories to tell for shock value. Even in the blazing heat, we slept with the windows closed after that. She read the messages the Egyptian man sent me late at night and told me I shouldn't always respond. We discovered a love of similar music and a comparable dry sense of humor. She understood.

And yet, even then, I couldn't always be entirely frank, partially out of fear of rejection. At night, we both sat in furiously charged silence, heads bent to the tasks of our individual journals. I appreciated her unexpected moodiness. Her quiet intensity perfectly matched my own. In these moments, I knew she was processing the world through her eyes. I liked her weirdness, and her weirdness recognized mine. She saw me, and I saw her. But still, I kept secret the changes in my mood and body. Every day, the work seemed to get longer and harder. This wasn't the escapist artist vacation I had once imagined it would be. I do not know where exactly the journal I kept during that time is now. Perhaps it is in one of the boxes where I store such things in my office? Or perhaps it was lost in the shuffle of a move? But to this day, I remember vividly hearing my own labored breathing as I wrote things down. My smoking increased (I went from an average of two to three cigarettes a day to clearing half a pack with ease.) My drinking spiked. I wasn't sleeping well and woke up early in the morning in a panic. My mind seemed to be slipping away from me the longer I stayed, and yet I still convinced myself this was what "real" artists do. They suffer. Habits and behaviors that were normalized in college and grad school (sleeping late, overworking, cramming, drinking copious amounts of caffeine, feeling shaky and unstable) were starting to become a shadow haunting my early adulthood. Coupled with working for our often careless and narcissistic director, my mental health had significantly declined since I'd arrived in this town. But I was determined not to waste this opportunity, so I held that part of my tongue and wrote it all down, keeping it secret even from (_____) though I suspected she'd understand.

* * *

One day our hostess offered to take (_____) and me to Perugia. Anxious for the variety of the city, I got ready in the morning with unprecedented glee. A day away from our small town! A day where I could walk through crowds and be pressed in on all sides by strange bodies. A day of anonymity. A day of variety. This is what I desired more than anything else after three weeks of non-stop working.

We are accompanied by a man who is an Italian teacher and a friend of our hostess. My roommate has never been one to waste words on small talk, but I am unexpectedly bursting at my seams with chatter. The teacher is trying to pass an English proficiency test and insists on speaking to us only in our native tongue. This is easy since neither (_____) nor I know more than a pocketful of guidebook Italian phrases. In my last week in Italy, I stick my hand into my suitcase and discover the Italian language dictionary my best friend from high school gave me the week before I left home. It has been untouched and all but forgotten, but when I find it after seven weeks of constant confusion, I smile to myself, remembering how furiously I clung to it during my eight-hour flight while trying to learn how to say at least a few words.

That day in Perugia, I try to explain to the teacher that I used to be a performer. I rarely say "actress," and to this day, I have no idea why. I perform. If people ask me, I say, "I've been performing since I was eleven." The man smiles at me and says, "Ah, an actress!" when I tell him about my work and my ongoing PhD research. We weave through the crowd, my roommate and I happy to be away from the confining ancient walls of the small town, to see strangers and hear a cacophony of languages. This city is not so big, but after weeks of rural life, it is my own sprawling metropolis.

I see a fountain up ahead and determine it's a great place to take a photo. I hand my camera to our guide and charge ahead, snaking through tourists studying the massive cathedral behind me. When I reach the fountain, I turn around to smile for the camera. But first, I look up at the fence surrounding the pool. With a flair for the dramatic, I grab a spoke and hoist myself onto the rim of the fountain, swinging around until my head is looking back over my shoulder. Our guide exclaims, "Such agility!" I see people around the base of the fountain smile at me with pleasure. I'm sure I look young and American and carefree and Black. I smile wider, my eyes hidden behind the frames of my large sunglasses. When I see the picture on the screen of my phone, I notice that the leg hanging over the edge of the fountain rim is about to lose its shoe. But I think it looks rather charming, like I've been swept off my feet in a Roman Holiday–style escapade.

My father has always explained that his tendency to be camera-happy stemmed from the fact that there are so few pictures of his childhood in Jamaica. At this point in my life, I've never seen a picture of my mother younger than eighteen or maybe sixteen years old. I saw a rare baby photo of my father once when I was twenty or twenty-one, but it lives in the house of a distant cousin, and we do not have a copy. On both sides of my family, there is a dearth of personal images. I do not know what my parents looked like as babies. I do not know what my grandparents looked like as young adults. Most of my aunts and uncles, cousins, grandparents, and parents seem to have been born as fully-grown people in my mind, suddenly coming into being at age eighteen, nineteen, or twenty when they gained access to cameras at universities or cities in Canada, the US, and the UK.

More than once friends have commented on me being particularly photogenic. I always wondered if it was a backhanded compliment, a way of telling me I look better on film than I do in real life. As I got older, I learned to accept the truth of what they were saying with grace. Part of this perhaps is due to being quite aware and used to being watched. Growing up in a Black family in an all-white neighborhood, attending a primarily white Catholic girl school I am quite used to observation, if mostly from a further distance than the edge of a camera lens.

In the town square in Perugia, I scan the crowd and see a man. He is thin and blond, dressed in a mismatched way that is supposed to make it clear to others that he is an artist. He has a thick mustache deliberately styled with waxy gel to mimic a period long past. He stands about three yards away from us, his camera trained in our direction, pointed at the level of our faces. The camera is large and professional, with a long-extended lens. I twist around to face him, and I feel the sunlight on the edges of my ribs as my cropped t-shirt begins to ride up right below my breasts, leaving a gap between its edge and the end of my high-waisted skirt. I shudder at the unexpected warmth and my lips part, stunned at this man's boldness. At that moment

I hear the camera click again and then quickly twice more. I
stand still.

At that moment, I can see those pictures in my mind. Me
smiling at my roommate, mouthing the lyrics of the song I
haven't heard in months being sung by women whose accents
I can't quite place. Me scanning the crowd, trying to locate
the source of the clicking noise. Me in the sunlight, my mouth
tipped open, and the small patch of my ribs exposed, caught
in a genuine, candid photo for the first time in years. My dark
brown face one of the few brown faces in the crowd. I imagine
the halo of my afro soaking up the light beaming down behind
my head, casting long shadows from the cathedral over my
shoulder. And in the final photo, my brows slightly furrowed
as I recognize what is happening, pointing at the man in
confusion and anger. I never thought of myself as a particularly
interesting subject, and later, I would wonder who the man
was and where the photo ended up. As the blond man lowers
his camera, looks at me, and then turns back into the crowd, I
know with almost certainty that I will never see that picture.
And this troubles me.

Later that day, we stand atop a rooftop lounge that looks
out over the city. I stand close to the edge with my stomach
pressed flush against the railing. Our guide stands directly
behind me, his small face close to my left shoulder, and points
straight across at the skyline, telling me that what I see are the
hills of Assisi. Being the fallen Catholic schoolgirl that I am, I
immediately recognize the name from Saint Francis. I vaguely
remember he did something with animals. We prayed to him
often. His name was usually tucked into the long list of saints,
public figures, and departed biblical characters we asked to pray

for us. Mary, Mother of God. Pray for Us. Pope John Paul.
Pray for Us. Saint Francis of Assisi. Pray for Us. There used to
be a special prayer for Francis we all had to memorize. I used
to know how to recite prayers in Latin as well. I've long since
forgotten those lessons. I turn to my roommate and ask her to
take my picture this time. First, I take one leaning against the
wall. Then I take one with my hostess, one with my roommate,
a few more with all three of us, and another with our guide.

For my last picture, I look at one of the pillars lining the
edge of the roof. I try to clamber up onto it but can't reach it.
My roommate kneels, and I slip my foot into her hand, landing
with a bounce onto the narrow seat of the pillar. I am terrified
of heights. But sitting above Francis's Assisi and still stunned by
my unexpected candid photo in the square, I am determined
to get the shot. I lean back into the sun and deploy my usual
tricks: I turn my face into the light, tilt my head to the side, and
smile directly into the camera over the harsh palpitations of my
heart.

When I see the picture later, I am glad that my terrified
hand clutching the edge of the stone pillar is rendered invisible
behind my back. I don't look anxious or afraid but rather
effortless and carefree. My photo doesn't show homesickness or
displacement. It doesn't show the everyday care, the sometimes-
stifling nature of the small town. The edge of my rib is peeking
out again from under my cropped t-shirt, displaying a very
small band of skin between its cuff and the waist of my skirt.
I feel proud that I've reclaimed this picture. I imagine it looks
at least close to the one that was stolen from me. We leave
Perugia and return to our hostess's car, which is parked in an
underground garage. We step onto an escalator traveling down

and I look up idly at the people on the escalator next to ours traveling the equivalent of three full flights of stairs in the opposite direction. I see a woman with an afro moving into the glare of the skyline, the first one I've seen in weeks. I let my eyes follow her upward progress, unashamed until I see her disappear from view.

* * *

We went to a festa later that night in a nearby town. We ate handmade pasta and watched older couples dancing on the square floor. (_____) and I stood at the edge of the crowd, swaying slightly and watching the movements in a sort of daze. When we both noticed an older Italian couple squinting at us from across the sea of dancers, (_____) leaned over and whispered in my ear, "Bet they think that you're my girlfriend. I wonder how many interracial gay couples have ever passed through this town?" I nearly choked to death laughing. We got in the car, full of food and wine, and returned to something approximating home.

* * *

For the first ten days I was in Italy I wore my hair in little twists. The day before I left my parents' house for two months of the unknown my mother sat with me between her legs for four painstaking hours, twisting each little strand first one time around and then once around again, until they formed a tight cap of bouncy curls. I enjoyed this momentary distraction and accepts the offer she makes every time I have to travel for extended periods of time. I know it soothes her to lay hands on me before I go. It soothes me too.

There's a certain infantilizing calm that washes over me when my mother braids my hair. I sit between her knees on the floor, enjoying the curious relaxation and closeness that comes from the rhythmic parting, greasing, and petting of the scalp, the agony of neck ache and backache, and the childish fidgety energy of being forced to sit so still.

On my tenth or eleventh day in Italy my head began to itch. It crept up slowly in the crown of my hair, radiating outward to the farthest edges. I covertly scratched it when I could, not wanting people to mistake my lack of hair washing for dirtiness, as white people so often have. I used to dread the question of why I didn't wash my hair everyday at childhood sleepovers, and I still rigorously avoid it now. I sat down on the floor of my bedroom to comb out my hair, chatting with (_____) while she painted her toenails light blue, her long blonde hair swinging down over one shoulder. The strokes of the paintbrush against her trimmed nails matched the scraping strokes of my bristle brush as I gently untangled the knots from my hair. We were both moving from root to tip.

I went about the innocuous activity in the usual self-deprecatory and overly apologetic fashion I've deployed whenever I have a white or non-Black roommate: "I'm sorry if I shed hair on the floor," "This will take a while," "The residue flakes are hair gel not dandruff," etc., etc. To my surprise she sort of shrugged, telling me she'd had a Black roommate before me and that she used to help her undo box braids with extensions. She laughed about how messy they can get (especially when you don't wash them) and we shared a moment of secret hair care intimacy I had only ever had with other Black women. In that instant I loved her.

She didn't ask me intrusively about my hair care regimen, about the products and tools of the trade I had spread out across the floor. She didn't make jokes about afro picks or laugh uneasily while staring openly. In fact, throughout the entire process her gaze remained steadfastly focused on her splayed wet toes, only glancing peripherally at my face and hair the few times she deigned to look up at me over the edges of her glasses.

I will always remember: until the day she left she was the only person who didn't try to pet my head. This made her very dear to me. Many people asked. Most did not and touched me anyway. Sometimes I even said yes.

One by one I unwound the little strands of hair. Twisting them through and around my index fingers and thumbs, using my middle finger to shake them loose. I carefully unpacked the hair care products I had bought in bulk and in advance before coming on this trip, knowing it would be extremely unlikely for me to find a suitable substitute abroad and that even if I did, I wouldn't be able to read the ingredients list. I laid them around me on the floor in a crescent moon, in the order that I would need them. Jars and combs and brushes and conditioners and oils and creams. They made me feel like a secret scientist or a kitchen sink chemist.

After the better part of an hour, I was finally done and headed into the bathroom. I washed my hair under the stream of hard water that I was convinced was making it dryer than the water back at home. When I emerged from the bathroom my hostess smiled at me and placed her hands next to her head, framing her face and moving them upwards in several degrees to signal "big hair". I smiled and said "Sì, grazie."

I grew very fond of the family I was staying with in the five weeks I was there. They were very warm and loving and perhaps what I pictured an Italian family to be. There was no man that lives in the house and it's bizarre to me that my image of the Italian family is so distinctly feminine. I'm not entirely sure why, but the family in my imagination is the same as the one I ended up living with: three generations of women, who sometimes argue and yell early in the morning and make four-course lunches at noontime and show affection with kisses on each cheek. I cannot tell now if my image of the family came before or after my stay here. Before or after my time in the little attic twin bedroom with (_____). Before or after the elderly grandmother washed my underwear in the sink when I left them behind in the bathroom with the sort of indifference to nudity and privacy only the very old seem to have.

* * *

In my time in Italy, I traveled through many cities: Perugia, Orvieto, Pavia, Milan, Florence, Rome. I spent one day in Lugano, Switzerland staring out at a big crystal lake. There is not much to do in that town except look into the windows of stores where I cannot afford the clothing. I heard a story about Oprah being turned away by a Swiss store clerk who assumed she couldn't afford an expensive handbag because she was Black. It is being hailed as some sort of international incident but by this time I am near the end of my trip, and I can no longer emotionally afford to focus all the time on the things I hear in the news. I didn't even know there are places in the world where people have never heard Oprah Winfrey's name or seen her beaming Black image.

While I was abroad the Trayvon Martin verdict was passed down. Not guilty. Because of the time difference and rehearsals that lasted long into the night, I did not hear about the story until many hours after the fact. I felt heavy-hearted and astonished at the continuation of American cruelty. I felt heavy that I didn't hear about it right when it happened. I went online and saw that my friends back home were taking to the streets. I wanted to take to the streets. It seemed unnerving to me that nothing seemed to change in the town around me. The Egyptian men were still displaced, laying bricks in the turn-around in the square. Trayvon was still murdered. And I was miles and miles away from home with no one to talk to about the aching that had developed between my eyes and deep down in the pit of my stomach.

I felt a sad heavy weight of Black suffering. It felt even heavier when I made up my mind to stop reading the headlines every day for the sake of my own sanity. I rotated every other day so I could take time off between the weightiness of things. It never really worked.

A Dirge for Girlhood

You have a penchant for telling true, sad stories.

Telling true stings like a lungful of inhaled ocean, salty but clean. Now that you are older, you wonder where else the salt is. Was salt there when you first taught your shame-filled fingers to explore your southernmost lips? When you were trying anxiously to remember the directions that you had carefully researched online, looking for medical diagrams instead of porn? (You always were a clinical child.) Directions on how to find your clitoris without a mirror and a diagram and a well-directed light?

Was salt there in your understanding of yourself as a budding sexual constellation? Was it there when you realized that your constellation's light was actually quite bright, visible not only to you but to other stargazers and sky mappers? That its pubescent shine made them uneasy in their ignorance? That some of them would one day bring you pleasure while others would bring immeasurable pain?

You are older and writing this when your sister comes in from spreading salt on the snowfall in the yard. She enters on a gust of winter, hands outstretched to show you how the salt has peeled away the protective layers of her palms' skin. You conclude that salt was there in your younger years, peeling away the flesh and preparing your ossified Black woman's bones inside the downy softness of your girlhood.

You know now that your girlhood is not tied up in your southernmost lips, or your clumsy exploration, or the taste of salt. Girlhood did not melt away from you the first time a man made a way inside you where there seemed to be only anxious possibility, darkness, and a well-directed light, as people had warned you when you were a child. Instead, girlhood was more like when you were younger and your mother would tell you that salt water had the power to gargle away the sickness from your throat. Girlhood was like that: both the sickness and the salt, coarse and refined, cause and cure. Preparing your tongue. Making room.

I.

You are younger. The same age you were when you discovered the shape of your body with a well-directed light, but still years away from admitting it. Eleven. You are changing for gym class and completing all sorts of clothing gymnastics to avoid exposing your bare skin. This maneuvering takes you longer than all of the other girls, and your best friend (loyal to a fault) stays behind to change with you. You are both bare-chested as babies with nothing to speak of in terms of breasts, but you still stand back-to-back with your chests curled inward while you hastily change your shirts. You stare at opposite concrete walls. You finish and make your way slowly across the lawn to the tennis courts, lagging far behind the other girls and laughing in the wind. You notice that your nipples, unbound by a bra, stand up proudly on your chest. You have never seen anyone else's nipples before, but you have already convinced yourself that yours are too large and, therefore, grotesque. You try to draw your shirt away from your offending chest when your best friend notices and laughs. She confesses that she feels strangely "womanly" when her nipples harden in the cold this way. You smile, love her, and agree. You both dawdle on the grass, eager to avoid tennis, pulling your white uniform shirts tighter and tighter against your chests, facing the wind, and laughing at the responsive nubs underneath. You wonder if everyone else in the world is standing somewhere near or far with their loyal best friends, thrusting their unformed breasts against a gym uniform shirt, facing the wind, and laughing at the hardened skin ridges forming under bleach-white cotton.

You ponder this question for years before any accusations of a womanish or "force-ripe" body are rained upon your head by strange men. Your breasts and hips refuse to come for years, and so do your menses. The only thing determined to grow on your body is your feet. And so you face the wind and laugh at the responsiveness of your nipples with a friend who is your best one, and you don't worry anymore about your baby-bare chest for many months. You wish now that you could have learned all the secrets of your body in this way: in the wind, laughing, next to your best friend, unembarrassed and unafraid.

II.

At age twenty-five, your psychiatrist jokes that every week you come in it feels like you've won some new prize or award or gotten some publication going. You laugh at that, knowing that he means well. But you also tell him, "I don't fuck people who care about me," and how this makes you feel dissociated from your body sometimes, even during sex. You say it's hard for you to love the people that you date. That sometimes they accuse you of ignoring them and that it is true. You say the guy you're with right now leaves messages on your phone and you can't feel bothered to answer him. When he left your bed last night, you were relieved because you like to sleep alone. Sometimes you pretend you like to cuddle (because you assume normal women do) but it actually makes you uneasy. You say all of this after the psychiatrist notes the prizes and publications, the conferences, the awards.

He pauses and then says that it's not your main problem. He'd rather you distance your emotions and remain measured in relationships rather than rushing in, falling in love, and becoming overly attached to every partner, like some of his other patients. You remember, "Only fools rush in." Isn't that the name of a song? You tell him about the Plan B you took before you came up to the appointment. This seems to shock him out of his reserve. You don't feel particularly compelled in either direction. The pill was just a fact. In your mind, it wasn't even a slightly offbeat fact since you've taken it a few times before, although it represented a departure from your usual carefulness with condoms. He tells you again not to worry about your detachment. Assures you that you are not cold. Then he lectures you on being "careful." You remind him that you run a fairly strict "no glove, no love" policy and ignore his furrowed brow. You wonder what his angle is. It seems like a pretty big problem that you can't fuck people you love. But if the doctor says not to worry about it, then you won't worry (yet).

You are five or six years old in the family room of your childhood home. Your dad is teaching you self-defense moves as the TV blares Nickelodeon cartoons in the background. He's asking you what you will do if someone tries to take you. You sigh, kind of bored with this same old question. "Scream, Daddy. I'll scream." And, he presses you, what else? "I'll fight. Draw attention. Won't let them put me in their car." You hear on *Oprah* when your babysitter is watching that your chance for survival is greatly reduced if you get moved from one location to another. You parrot this fact back to your father while surreptitiously trying to watch *Rugrats* on TV. Years later, you wonder if your friends in other houses received the same education. Now comes part two. "Try to break my hold," your father says, grabbing your skinny wrist.

You wrench your arm backward against his thumb, so hard it would break the finger if he didn't let go (or so you imagine). This is your favorite part. You like wrenching your wrist this way and that way. You like wrestling with Dad because you know that at the end he will give you an airplane ride, throwing you up in the air, and tickling your face with his beard. You have never been afraid of your father. You just like feeling strong against your six-foot-two, two-hundred-plus pounds maker. He tells you for the millionth time about a boy from the news. How he was almost snatched off the street on his way home from school by a man he did not know in the Bronx. He tells you how the boy saved his own life because he fought back, because he made noise, because he ran. "You've got to fight," he tells you. "Don't let them take you." After showing you a few more moves and delivering the highly anticipated airplane ride, he leaves you alone with the TV and the cartoons again.

You are maybe eleven or twelve years old, and your father won't let you go to a friend's house because he does not know her father. The same friend who stood with her nipples in the wind in gym class. Your best friend. He gets upset because they want to take you to the beach and ask you to bring a swimsuit. What if you drowned? You are not a strong swimmer. You don't know her father either, but you want to go swimming at the beach, a beach filled with salt and sand, not chlorine like the public swimming pools at the YMCA. The same pools that the male lifeguard at the YMCA with two nipple rings always told you would turn bright red and burn your legs if you peed in them. Your parents don't care much for American beaches with their cigarette-butt-filled sand and their murky brown water. After you see the crystal blue oceans in their native Jamaica, you somewhat understand their aversion to their American counterparts. But that day when you are eleven or twelve years old, you want to go to the beach, and you cry in angry protest.

Later that same year, you spend hours on the computer with another new friend. You both make up an alter ego named "Tyler," who is a blond surfer from California. You and your friend use a made-up AOL profile to talk to strangers as "Tyler," and you both imagine that you are skilled at talking sexy like a sixteen-year-old blond boy surfer from California would. You message people in anonymous chat rooms. "A/S/L?" "Age/sex/ location?" You type this and wait for the ping of a response.

Sometimes, you rub your old Barbie dolls together in a plastic simulation of passionate love while you wait. You do this mostly at her house, in the seclusion of the basement, because your parents are far too strict and attentive to leave you alone with a computer. She speaks with false authority as she smashes the dolls together. "This is how it is," she tells you. "This is how you *do it.*" Her voice always has a little hitch in it when she says, "*Do it.*" It's the same tone she uses to ask you at least once a week at lunchtime with probing curiosity if you've gotten your period yet. The same tone she uses to convince you to practice "pretend making out" in the back of her mother's minivan one day when you are left alone again. Your factual parents have told you the biological logistics of sex, but it seems like a ludicrous hypothetical to you. You look at the smooth doll genitals and wonder what "*doing it*" would mean. The front side looks similar to yours: smooth, flat, and hairless. It's the underneath that makes you most confused since that's where it seems everything of import will happen to you. And in your thinking, sex is something that just happens, not something you do. When your vagina begins to prickle with hair and transform from resembling the smooth doll parts, you laugh at it in the mirror, thinking the front side at least looks oddly similar to your newly developing armpits.

You don't trust your friend's advice or her demonstration with the dolls. But this is the same friend who convinced you that year to eat dog food and to taste berries off a potentially poisonous bush on the edge of the schoolyard. She had all the bravado of ignorance and the willpower of a child. So, you smash the dolls together, think it looks painful, and wait for the loud ping of responses online.

Later that same year or around the same time, your father sits you down with a flyer that came to the house in the mail. It has the names and pictures of every registered sex offender in your town organized by zip code. Your town is pretty much segregated along class and race lines. You notice a lot of the men are Black and live downtown. You say this out loud. Your father says that you shouldn't let this fool you and that it isn't representative of the truth. He tells you that there are more than that, white ones and other ones that just haven't been caught yet but will hurt you. Try to hurt you. You learn when you are older about violence and how widespread it is, that it isn't blind to race or class. That these things happen everywhere, that some places and people just hide it, or don't go to jail, or don't get caught because they have money and privilege. Or because they get away with shit that they shouldn't. That the violence doesn't start neatly downtown or end uptown. That the flyers don't show everything. That's what he was trying to tell you. You do not understand what he was saying until you are older, much older. At the time you shift anxiously in your chair at the dining room table, eager to do anything else in the world. You miss the times before this when you were blissfully unaware of the violence around you. You wish for that ignorance to return, to wash over your body like waves at the beach. To fill your lungs, body, and brain with the peace that ignorance alone can provide.

But you won't pretend here that you knew how to articulate that then. You just notice and don't know. You practice the wrist-grabbing trick a few more times. Catch and release. Catch and release. You are too big now for an airplane ride. You do not miss the beach so much after that.

III.

Now you are older (much older, twelve years older, twenty-four) and you are outside having a cigarette. You always seem to have at least one vice. It is raining but you are mostly protected under the awning that makes your red brick apartment building look like decorated gingerbread on the best of days. This is not one of those days. It is night. A man approaches you in a drenched windbreaker, head bowed into the gusts of rain, black hood pulled down low over his eyes. The fabric makes a swishing sound every time his arms rub up against his sides. He stops in front of your steps to ask you for a cigarette, and you notice it is the first time in a long time that you haven't flinched when a strange man addresses you in the dark. You don't flinch or panic or feel much of anything at all. You forgot the rest of the pack inside and you tell him so. He asks you for the one in your hand and you offer him the ash end. Your fingers briefly touch in the transfer, but still no flinch, no panic, nothing much at all. He sucks hungrily at the place where your mouth used to be, and you watch him enjoy the hit with a sense of germaphobic unease. Doesn't he know your mouth, a stranger's mouth, used to breathe there? Doesn't he know that he doesn't know you at all? You remember once in college when you were all broke one of your friends drank all the leftover half-filled glasses on empty tables in the bar to get drunk and it worked. You figure this isn't quite as bad as that. You scorn yourself internally for being condescending towards this man.

He brings his brown face real close and asks you for a dollar to go with his cigarette. You don't have a dollar, not even your wallet. You didn't even bring the cigarette pack. You show him your pockets, empty except for your keys. He believes you because it is true, tucks his brown face back under the black hood and walks away in the rain with your cigarette butt warming his hands. His arms continue to make that steady swishing sound over the patter of the rain. You watch him go.

When you are younger (not much younger, three years younger, barely twenty-one years old) you are in the popular college bar. Popular for its cheap drinks and loose policy around IDs and crowded dance floors and loud loud (painfully loud) music that reverberates into the very center of your chest until you feel like you are ready to move or shake apart. The white man with no shirt on your left is a hair too close and you notice that your friends are far away. You ask in a voice straining to be heard above the music in the hollow of his ear if he can give you some space. He responds by slamming you back against the cement brick wall on the edges of the dance floor, caging you in on all sides with his arms and bare chest, and repeating the words, "There is no room. There is no room here." The "here" falls heavy on your ringing eardrums and tender head, and you wonder why you left the house that night with friends who are now far away, and you aren't that close to anyway and who can do nothing to protect you. You scan the crowd for your one close friend, your best friend, but he is far away too, and you can't see him over the arms and bare chest in front of you, and you can feel the panic rising in your throat because there is no room. Here.

You always assumed when you were little and watching cartoons that people wouldn't fuck with you, that they'd know through some kind of osmosis that your dad would kill them. This dude is caging you in and snatching at your wrists. You feel the sting on your spine where your back and skull connected with the wall. Your instinct is telling you to fold in on yourself, to wait it out and hope to heaven for an intervention, either from your far-away, out-of-sight friends or a stranger. Your Dad's voice is telling you to fight. To break his hold. To fight fight fight. To scream even if they can't hear it on the dance floor with the low-down lights and the loud loud music. This man is getting closer to you now, his face a breath away from yours. He smells like alcohol and anger. Curling fingers into palms made slippery with sweat you make two fists and drive one straight into his chest, right above his heartbeat, and suddenly there is air and room here, there, and everywhere as he struggles to catch his breath. And you are free. You run away.

You drunkenly decide to stay in the bar. Later that night you are dancing somewhere else on the dance floor, and you feel a hard thump in the back of your head. A hard thump shaped like a fist. You wonder to yourself why you didn't just go home. Maybe because going home felt like a defeat, felt scared and small. You were the strong one. Your parents often noted when you were a child that you rarely cried when you fell down. You spent that night in the bar worrying that the shirtless white man would come back to retaliate and now he has. You turn around but you are unsteady and drunk and blindingly angry. You want to fight him in earnest now. You want to scratch him down until he's just a stain on the dance floor. Kill him. Obliterate him. Humiliate him. You want to survive him. Your best friend sees your face, reads your mind, and firmly leads you off the dance floor and out the front door of the bar. You had not told him or the friends that you had come with about the sting in your spine or the punch up against the wall of the bar. All he hears is you stutter the words, "I think that guy just hit me." He does not know who the guy is, so he takes you home, tells you to go to sleep. You go home to your dorm and don't cry. You sleep like the dead.

Now you are older (one year older, but still twenty-one) and you are in another club in Philly. Out with a group of girls that you don't know that well. In fact, you don't know them at all. They are all pretty, bad, Black and brown girls and they know it. Bad like the girls on TV. Bad like the women you imagine men want. Bad like women who know they're beautiful and aren't waiting on your approval to make it true. They take up the very center of the dance floor, sending scornful looks to the men they deem unattractive and inviting ones to the guys they think can hang. You stand awkwardly in your new short dress on the periphery, envying their confidence but feeling pretty damn good. You do not know how this is supposed to work yet, but you start to dance, moving your hips in small circles and smiling at your new crew. The music is loud and pulsing, and you really start to get down. You feel the other bad girls grab your hands and pull you further into the circle. You figure this is a sign that you can hang, and you like it. Men circle the perimeter and soon each girl is moving with a partner. You fall back a little bit until you are in the second layer of the circle, where the men pressed against the backs of the pretty, bad, Black and brown girls are standing. You are smiling and moving on your own, eager to feel the music in this crowded club you've never been to.

Suddenly you feel two firm hands grab your hips from behind and pull. You come into contact with the solid wall of a body curved around you. There's a hard erection in the crease of your ass and you freeze. He is not welcome. You break free of the man's grasp, you never see his face, just the Black skin of his hands and the blunt tips of his nails as his fingers struggle to hold on to you. Doesn't he know that your dad will kill him? Doesn't he know that? Why doesn't he know that? You realize in this moment that he doesn't care. That most people do not care. That the shirtless white guy in the bar didn't care. That having a father or a brother or a boyfriend or a friend does not make you immune. That is what they know. And now you know it too.

You run out of the circle, breaking through the dancing couples, trying to get as far away from his hard dick as you possibly can. Your one friend, the one person you know well from the group of pretty, bad, Black and brown girls, follows you and asks what's wrong. You swallow your tongue, embarrassed by some stranger's dick, blaming yourself. Say in a small voice so none of the pretty, bad, Black and brown girls will hear you, "I want to go home." You go home in a cab by yourself.

When you are six or seven years old, your mama, president of her law school's Black Lawyers Association, teaches you your Miranda rights. Tells you what to do if the police ever take you. She tells you not to fight, to go. Let them take you; don't give them any excuse to kill you (Even though you both know this doesn't always work.) She says to take their names and badge numbers. She especially emphasizes your right to remain silent. You have a right to remain silent. You have exercised this right for many years.

Now you are twenty-two, and you are in the popular grad school bar. A drunken white woman with skinny limbs and flowing, curly black hair purposely throws a cup of water into the crowd. It bounces off the back of your head before flowing down your hair and back, the plastic less perceptible than the water. You turn to her. She tries to put her arm around you like a friend. This feels like the final straw. You tell her not to touch you anymore, to get away from you. You tell her you are mad about the water. She smiles hazily and continues to hold you in the circle of her limp arm. She does not apologize. You tell her again to get away from you. At first, you are whispering it, but then you're screaming, "GET THE FUCK AWAY FROM ME." Your hand is held up like a stop sign, and you are not silent. You repeat the words over and over again, knowing in your heart that your rising anger has as much to do with her as it does with that hard thump you felt on the back of your head in the college bar with the cheap drinks and loose policy around IDs and the man in the bar with the bad Black and brown girls. You are tired of the disrespect, of being touched out of turn, and of being treated carelessly. You are mad at this woman who assumed she could throw water on you and not apologize. You are mad she assumed you could be friends. Your new grad school friends tell you not to fight white people, especially white women, in public anymore. Tell you they'll kick you out of Yale for shit like that, because who would believe you over her. Your family agrees. No one defends your right not to be treated carelessly. And you learn.

Then you are twenty-four and having a panic attack in a club in New York City. You push past this little dark-skinned Black dude trying to chat up a white woman. You put your hand in between his shoulder blades and apply pressure so you can slip by him. You are desperate to get to the door. You think later to yourself that lots of little dudes who are short and overcompensate by working out too much look like big muscular thumbs. He starts with you, pulling on the back of your jacket and yelling in your ear. He's calling you bitch, calling you names, calling you "Hey you with the aaaa-fro!", insulting your hair. He's pulling your jacket, calling you *bitch*, "Hey you with the aaaaa-fro!" You round on him and scream, "WHAT DID YOU SAY TO ME YOU BALD-HEADED BITCH? YOU GOT SOMETHING TO SAY TO ME YOU BALD-HEADED BITCH?" You don't know where the words come from, but you give him back *bitch* because that's what he's called you, and all of a sudden, it's on and you can't stop it. You get this hitch in your voice every time you say *bitch*, since that seems to be working the most on him. You can tell the dude is scared of you and your anger, so you mirror his aggression and make yourself bigger, angrier, and more out of control. You want him to be scared. He deserves to be scared. You call him a bitch again. Then your friend is throwing his body in between the two of you and the bouncer is telling you that you have to leave the club and you keep cursing and crying and screaming until you're on the other side of the door where you desperately wanted to be in the first place. And then you're apologizing to everyone in your group for ruining their night. You tell them that you're triggering, that this dude was gaslighting you, that you lost control. And they don't blame you. They say they understand, even though you can't let yourself believe them.

IV.

Now you are twenty-one (barely twenty-one, after the club where your back hit the wall), and you are about to let a man put his penis inside of you for the first time. You know this is a clinical way of describing losing your virginity, but it's the best description you have. You've seen one before and handled it, but you've never let it inside of your privacy. You tell him to put on a condom. He asks you if you're a virgin, and you say no because you don't feel like one. He is a complete stranger that you took home from a bar. You laugh when you see him naked, which makes him turn pink with a furious blush that spreads all over his face. You've never seen an uncircumcised penis before, and you tell him that you think it looks like a pink tube sock rolled up for the drawer. You have always had a penchant for saying the exact wrong thing. He blushes harder and all over, and you can see it because he is bare. You feel ready to do this, but right before he enters you, you angle your hips away and stop him with a hand on his chest, right above his heartbeat. "I'm putting a lot of trust in you right now." He looks surprised and urgent like he just wants to put his white and pink tube sock penis inside of you. Says he knows.

That night you remember that one time on a dance floor at your first college party, aged eighteen, a boy put his teeth into the meat of your shoulder, coming up to you from behind. Told you that you were both drunk and that you would have sex with him based on that fact alone. You told him you were not drunk and flinched away from the sharp set of his teeth. You tell this story as a joke to many friends, although it keeps you from sleeping some nights because you think it is strange and you worry you may see him again on campus. You also think that it is a rare fact. Something like this will never happen to you more than once in your lifetime.

You whisper again to this man in your bed who, a scant hour ago, was a stranger exhaling a cigarette outside of an unknown bar. The man and the bar share the same smoky smell and anonymous friendly air.

"I'm putting a lot of trust in you."

-

The Rules of the Game

"But what does it *mean?*"

Seven or eight years old, I pulled the boy with dark skin like mine into the farthest, darkest corner of the cubby room near the back door of our second-grade classroom. It was during the time between when we returned from recess and before our afternoon "meditation" (which to a group of overtired children usually turned into an impromptu nap). But in that moment coming in from the playground I could have sworn I heard him say something that sounded like "gaga." This is what he swore he said when our white teacher, her face full of blood and outrage, swooped down on us. With a tremor in her voice that sounded like thunder, she threatened to send him "straight to the principal's office" if he had "really said what I think you said!"

With her tall stature and airy way of talking, her jet-black hair interrupted by one long, thick white streak she referred to as her "skunk stripe," I was surprised to see her so transformed by a mere utterance. After all, the word "gaga" wasn't in my seven- or eight-year-old lexicon, so surely it must not exist? My teacher's million pieces of jewelry began to flutter along with the floor-length bohemian skirt that she wore over her ample hips. Her oft-sported smile slid slowly from her face. Her reaction to this barely muttered word was so visceral; it was as if this little boy had reached up to pull out her skunk stripe while slapping her firmly from cheek to cheek. It was the first and only time I had ever heard her raise her lyrical voice.

What was this word with the power to make my favorite teacher, the first person on the face of this earth who told me I was a writer, ignite so quickly? What spark could be lit by baby talk? Could "gaga" be a new bad word? Naturally, now I was dying to know.

My parents fostered in me an obsession with etymologies. If I didn't know the definition of a word, out came the dreaded red-covered, Bible-thin pages of Merriam-Webster's attempt to catalog every word in the English language. If the word wasn't in English (Jamaican Patois being their native tongue), then I was in for double torture. I would have to not only look up the word but sit and listen to my father trace its origins. This ritual led me to adopt a policy of guerilla girl knowledge finding. I would wait until the adults were distracted (my mother chopping food in the kitchen, my father drinking his coffee in front of the news, my godmother cleaning the couch cushions, my aunties having a "big people" conversation) to spring my favorite question on them: "What does _____ mean?" This tactic was effective approximately 50% of the time until my father wised up to my trick and began storing up the words I had asked about during the day for nighttime. Then, I would be forced to look up all the words I'd queried about during the day in one fatal blow.

So, in that moment I was pressing a little seven-year-old boy into the farthest, darkest corner of the cubby room, not to exchange secretive childhood kisses, but to do the other thing spaces like these were made for: trading in "bad" words. His name likely started with a *J*, but I cannot remember now exactly what people called him back then. I do recall fondly the way he walked with his big pant legs in a deliberately wide stance, his hair cut into the kind of Pink Lotion-soaked haircut that R&B artists made popular in the mid to late '90s. This haircut and wide stance, in combination with his mother's love of coating his lips and the lower half of his face in too much Vaseline every morning, made me think at the time that he looked more like a miniature man rather than a little boy. Although the sweetness in his voice and the softness of his demeanor made him my peer in every way. He was a boy, not a miniature man. He was no more a man than I was a miniature woman. But in that moment in the cubby, he knew something that I didn't and that was a thing that my inner know-it-all could not stand. I had heard the mumbled "gaga" and I knew there was more there to mine, so I kept digging until he yielded under my probing gaze.

I waited. I was a little bit larger and more aggressive than he was, so I used these tactics to my advantage, the hierarchies of childhood well at play. There are rules to every game. Using my body to block his hasty retreat (Clearly, he was scared of being discovered again whispering the dreaded "gaga.") he finally conceded defeat. First, he looked left and then he looked right, in a gesture that suggested the cubby block was hot. Finally, he looked me square in the eye and said only in half a whisper, "Nigga."

I looked back at him in wide-eyed amazement, my little mouth (also bearing the signs of too much Mama-applied Vaseline) agape. In my pressed brown corduroy pants and yellow turtleneck, I felt too uncool to admit that I had no idea what this word meant, let alone that I had never used it before. I feigned insider status with a careless shrug, saying it must have been something like 'damn' or 'bitch.' I gave him the two 'bad' words I had learned from my family's womenfolk in exchange for his 'nigga.' Like trading cards, I assumed that my two bad words trumped his one. Rolling his eyes he said that it was nothing like that and instead offered me his own two-pronged etymology:

1) Nigger: (pronounced Nig-ger) a bad word white people call Black people.

2) Nigga: (pronounced Nigg-uh) a word his menfolk call each other. Something like a friend.

An alternately brash and quiet girl child, I was usually banished from the curious spaces of the barbershop, or the smoke-filled, alcohol-fueled basement of my uncles' gatherings. The only time these rules were broken was on the rare occasion I was allowed to follow my father for his haircuts and when my godmother allowed me to play dominos with her and the men on family holidays. An expert player, she would perch me on the edges of her knees to let me "play" her hand which usually consisted of her figuring out everyone else's moves less than five

minutes into the game and instructing me how to block my
uncles' plays, much to their chagrin and my delight. Tiny hands
gripping the smooth-backed pieces, I'd giggle as she whispered
the secrets of the game into the hollow of my ear. My favorite
part of this ritual was seeing her sweep the game, her excited
cries of "Hit dem, Dan Dan!" my cue to slam the dominoes
as hard as I could onto the fold-out table, rattling the other
players' pieces like teeth chattering in fear.

This brief moment of getting to mirror the Caribbean
masculinities that surrounded me every day thrilled me to no
end, the sharp sting of the dominoes radiating from my small
palms into the pit of my belly, where my godmother's firm
hand rested to prevent me from toppling to the floor in my
excitement to reach the farthest edges of the table. I'd slap the
table hard, looking back at her for approval, before using my
tiny girl hands to scoop up our winnings (quarters, if anything,
since the games were primarily played for stakes of gloating and
old-school braggadocio).

My own father, a more reserved man who neither drinks,
nor smokes, nor runs around on his wife, nor anything
particularly interesting, always forbade me from entering
spaces he deemed too "locker room-ish" for his inquisitive girl
child, especially as I was prone to excellent acts of inconvenient
mimicry.

I wondered in awe that day if nigga was there in the
sudden silence that often descended on the male spaces of the
barbershop and the domino game as soon as my little Black girl
body entered the room unannounced. I wondered if nigga was
there, living inside my father's and uncles' mouths or held back

against their teeth, somewhere deep down where they stored all the secret things that they kept hidden from me. I wanted more than the kitchen sink secrecy of my mama and aunties, which I was only allowed on the periphery of anyway. I wanted to know the downstairs secrets, the men's gathering secrets, the basement secrets, and I wondered silently if somehow nigga was the key that would spring open the locked doors of Black male life that my girl status could not. As I grew older, I recognized that nigga was more prevalent in the US than in my parents' native Jamaica, a thing that marked me as a Yankee cousin even more than my American accent and love of box mac and cheese. Even now, when I say it, it tastes different in my mouth than other words. Its flavor is both familiar and alien, like a fruit that is reminiscent of other things I've eaten before while bearing its own unique sweetness.

So this boy with the Pink Lotion hair and Vaseline lips and chin had done me a real solid. He gave me something I wasn't even aware was missing from my vast lexicon of American Blackness. He also unconsciously allowed me to glean two things in the deepest, darkest, furthest corner of the cubby room:

1) Nigger was a word that had the power to make white people extremely angry. In fact, it held a sort of inexplicable sway over their undulating emotions, something that seemed far outside the bounds of my seven-year-old Black logic.

2) If this little boy with the likely *J* first name was a nigga then I wanted to be a nigga too. He had also done me a favor so I decided that he was my nigga, and that

we would be united from this day forth in perpetual niggaship and live forever in niggadom, if such a thing truly existed.

So, this little boy was now my nigga. On the playground, we played and acted bad. I mirrored his wide-hipped gait and little hand gestures, the way he'd open his arms wide when he talked, and his tenderness around little Black girl children. The day another boy in my class charged me head-on during a game of tag, smacking me hard on the back until I crumbled, hands and knees and face rushing to meet the blacktop, my nigga helped me. He lifted me gently under each armpit when he realized my palms were too bloody and raw to grasp his hands. He wasn't a snitch, but when he jerked his small, pointed chin at the boy in question, the one who had been my attacker, I thought to myself for the first (and certainly not the last) time in my life, "I'm gunna *marry* this nigga."

Perhaps I should stop here to say a few words about my playground attacker.

At least twice my weight, with a short mop of straight brown hair and very rosy cheeks, he was the first white Jamaican I had ever met. Upon hearing his proclamation that "my mother is from Jamaica too" I didn't miss a beat or a hot second before telling him that Jamaicans couldn't be white because all Jamaicans were Black. This became the basis of a mildly adversarial beef between the two of us, that climaxed that day on the playground when cliques stood divided. It remained unresolved until the day his mother met my father. Looking at her face I saw something there that was recognizable but still I remained confused as my dark-skinned father laughingly exchanged Patwah words with this giantess of a white woman. It was the day I learned the phrase "Jamaica White."

1) Jamaica White: someone who can "pass," but everyone knows has a little Black in them somewhere.

2) Jamaica White: a white person from the island of Jamaica.

After the great counsel of the elders and a firm lecture from my father, the beef was squashed, and my former attacker became my nigga too.

* * *

When I was almost five years old we moved from our apartment in the Bronx to a home in New Rochelle. For many years we were the only Black family or family of color on our street.

Before we moved, I went to a school where everybody, including the teachers, children, and staff were either Jamaican or first-generation Jamaican Americans and Black. My church was Jamaican and Black. My block was Jamaican and Black. Until white faces suddenly surrounded me, I assumed that everyone in the entire world was Jamaican and Black. This was a safe assumption since to me the world stretched only as far as the hospital where my mother worked on one side, on another to the park near my home, on still another side to the grocery stores where we took our weekly trips, and lastly to my school. This small radius of the Northeastern Bronx, sometimes known as "The Valley," was the extent of my childhood consciousness.

It never occurred to me that there could be much more beyond this West Indian enclave. And why would it have? I was four years old.

New Rochelle, to me, seemed vast and wide. The first day we arrived in the hubbub of the movers and the mixture of cousins and aunties and uncles and commotion, I slipped out of the front door and through the hedges, getting lost on my way to the backyard. Convinced in my four-year-old mind that if I walked for long enough, I would see the old playground with its fountains that sprouted up out of the ground, or the ice cream truck that stayed on the corner, or my little school, or a neighbor's face to guide me home, I kept walking.

I grew tired and hot in the fall sun, so I picked up a stick, swinging it boldly like a sword, slashing the air first left then right. I pretended I was a Power Ranger and spoke to my invisible companions, goading and leading them on. I passed many strange white adult faces on the street, who looked at my unaccompanied four-year-old body with curiosity but did not try to stop me or ask me if I needed help. I did not find this strange at the time: Why should people in this new place know who I am? It is only now with the reflection of age that I marvel at how little they cared then. I cannot lie: I stand in dangerous hindsight judgment at the blind eyes of my new "neighbors."

At least an hour had gone by. I was growing scared even though my father and mother always told me I was brave. I used my stick to strike the ground three or four times like Moses did in my Sunday school reader, and imagined the concrete pavement parting before me like the Red Sea. At this moment, I saw a white woman in a white shirt standing in front of a white house. She was smoking a cigarette, which she flicked into the gutter before she came over to ask me if I was lost. I told her yes, my tentative "Yes" the first time I realized the truth inherent in the meaning of the word "Lost." Recognizing my helpless position, I placed my hand within hers after I had discarded the stick against the softly manicured grass of her front lawn. She led me inside a house I later described to my mother as "dirty," but I believe this was due to the fact that she had a love of white furniture and indoor pets. I lay on my belly next to her blond-haired grandson or godson (I cannot clearly recall which she said at the time.) and watched The Lion King on VHS. Giving her my phone number in the Bronx, she went to call Mommy and Mommy was crying on the phone. When she heard I was gone she had fainted, but my father told her to remain there since it was unlikely I would know the new number at the house in New Rochelle.

One of my cousins (not related) came to get me in the mover's cherry-red convertible with a white stripe down the side. There were dusty tarps and boxes in the car, but I did not mind. I sat on this big dark-skinned boy in his late-teens lap, and he was cradling me a bit too tightly in his arms, although I was sure he thought I did not notice. He and everyone at the house was scared when I was lost and I figured he was glad that I returned but embarrassed to admit this as a teenage boy. I ate the M&M candies that the woman had given to me as I was leaving, and enjoyed the sensation of my first convertible ride, the little bow-bows my mother had placed meticulously in my hair that morning clacking against the ends and tops of my braids as the wind rushed past my overheated cheeks.

When we reached the house, I was lifted up above the crowd of adults like a returning hero and I laughed with glee. My aunt was disheveled to the point of near mania, kissing my cheeks and bouncing me like the world's biggest Christmas package. I was passed from hand to hand and congratulated like a fabled conqueror, which only further reinforced my Power Ranger/Moses fantasies from the streets. We searched for the woman's house for many months after my safe return but were never able to locate the right one. I think this is largely because my parents underestimated just how far I had walked over the course of the long hour or more. It took me years to realize that in those hours I was lost my family believed:

1) That I had been kidnapped and not lost.

2) That one of my white neighbors had likely snatched me off the street.

Maybe it had to do with the fact that we were strangers in a strange land? Who knows? I certainly don't. All I knew and still know is what I said when I emerged from the car and was lifted high into the air: "I wish I could get lost every day so that I could get candy!"

In our early months living there the house was big and beautiful and empty, a small apartment's worth of furnishings forced to stretch out over the seemingly endless expanse of two floors, a basement, and five bedrooms. As I got older and we filled it to the rafters with the remnants of living, I recognized that the space was not so vast after all but rather a finite place that I can now traverse easily with my eyes closed.

The day my father paid the mortgage he told us with pride we would never be homeless (as long as we paid the property taxes). The house now belonged to us even when I felt like my body didn't belong in our neighborhood.

* * *

In New Rochelle, we walked to school. About half of the school walked and half of the school bused in from downtown, a conscious effort made by the school district to racially integrate every classroom in the 1960s. I learned two things from watching the "yellow bus kids" come to school earlier than me every morning:

1) If you could walk to school, you were most likely:
   a. White
   b. Middle class or upper-middle class
   c. Both

2) If you took the bus to school, you were most likely:
   a. Black or Latino/a
   b. Eligible for free breakfast and lunch
   c. Both

The answer to both questions was always *C* with very few exceptions. My siblings and I were one of the exceptions. My sister and I walked to school, living less than five minutes away from the doors of our classrooms. At the time I envied the yellow bus kids because they always arrived first to school and were first in the lunch line. As a result, they usually got dibs on all of the chocolate and strawberry milk before I got to the front. I never cared for the chalky almost medicinal taste of strawberry milk, but chocolate milk seemed like a precious commodity. I thought to myself, 'It must be great to ride all together to school every day and drink as much chocolate milk as you want before anyone else can join the line.' I did not understand what class was. I did not know what a free lunch program was and how it worked. I only knew that all the kids in my neighborhood were white, and all of my friends who looked like me were from downtown and not white.

When I visited their homes, I saw the insides of buildings housing many people. I only knew that this was where my friends who looked like me lived. They came to my house and poked around my single bedroom with curiosity. One of them lived in an area our town tried to condemn so that it could build an IKEA. White residents from my side of town complained that the excessive number of cars from a big box store would cause too much noise and pollution, thereby devaluing their property. IKEA never came. In the home of this friend, I ate my first Mexican food. Her mother laughed at me during a multicultural assembly because I tried to eat the corn husk around the tamale.

By fourth grade and after my friends visited my house, some days they played a game. They all pretended that they had a party over the weekend, speaking loudly about it in front of me until I hung my head low to cover the tears caused by their make believe. During these years I developed a strong taste for white milk, largely because it was the only thing left by the time I reached the front of the lunch line. And this was on the rare days that my mother allowed me the treat of buying the unpalatable school lunches with my friends instead of carrying one in my lunchbox from home. I glutted myself on white milk, sometimes having two or three containers in a row, causing me to ignore my lactose intolerance for many years until after I finished college.

My white friends from my neighborhood came to our home and asked my parents to speak in Jamaican accents and often refused to eat our food. They asked me why my voice sounded different when I spoke to my friends from downtown.

I decided in fifth grade to join the step team. On the team, I learned a bit of rhythm and camaraderie. I also learned that the only thing purportedly worse than acting like a white girl, or thinking I was a white girl, or dressing like a white girl, or talking like a goddamn white girl, was being a damn snitch. I guessed I had forgotten the lessons I had learned from my niggas in second grade. After absentmindedly telling our teacher that some of the girls didn't want to come to practice because they were outside playing, some days I was socially dead, forced to wander the playground alone because no one would talk to me. This policy was strictly enforced and policed by some girls and I accepted my punishment without complaint. I stayed close to the other social exiles, talking quietly to myself and making up games. Those days weren't so bad, except for my burning desire for my friends who looked like me to talk to me. But even a ten-year-old could understand the logic of the game.

* * *

During those social exile years, I got into the first (and only) physical fight of my lifetime with a boy I will call E. When we got to the third grade, we were divided up into class tracts based on standardized test scores. The classes were hierarchical in nature, starting with special education and

sloping upwards until the "gifted" class our school district
named "Kaleidoscope." The teachers assured us that there
was nothing wrong with being in any particular class, but we
all knew through their actions that they didn't believe that.
They often doted on the kids from Kaleidoscope, who got to
do things like run the school store, go on special field trips,
raise butterflies, and read Shakespeare when (more often than
not) they only paid attention to the kids in special education
to reprimand them or get them in trouble. Almost everyone
in special education came from downtown, and all the kids
in Kaleidoscope were from uptown. I was the only Black girl
or girl of color in my Kaleidoscope class. This was a subject
position and phrase I would repeat all the way through high
school, college, and sometimes even grad school. The role of
"only Black girl in ____" was like a part you never wanted to be
asked to play. I didn't want to be the only anything anywhere.

E was a large (for his grade and age) dark-skinned boy in
special education. Although our homeroom classes were mixed
and assigned at random, we always separated into five hierarchal
modules for math and reading. No one ever told us which class
was "gifted" and which was not. But we saw the answers in our
teachers' movements and demeanor, in the way some kids got
butterflies and others got detention. We watched and figured
out the rankings of classes all on our own. Oftentimes, white
teachers would ask me why the other Black children couldn't
be "good" like me. Good was code for quiet and scared of
authority. I felt ashamed that I was singled out from my peers
and made to feel special by putting them down. But I also
liked raising butterflies and reading Shakespeare, and running
the school store. I grew up rather ambivalent about these
differences, knowing on some level they were wrong and yet

accepting them as fact anyway. I didn't know why my teachers'
exceptionalism bothered me so much until I was old enough
to have language about racism and classicism. But by then, it
was too late to defend any of my classmates. Too often, the way
people talk about us determines the ways we view ourselves.
So, while I was busy in Kaleidoscope, my peers in special ed
were learning that they were less valuable, less "special," and less
worthy of good things because of our teachers' behavior. I regret
it now even though I didn't have the power to change it back
then.

The day E approached me and my friends on the
playground, writing in our notebooks during our self-appointed
"poetry club," things between us had been fraught for many
years. We were frequently paired together during homeroom so
that I could help him with his schoolwork. I think this pairing
must have bothered him since the unspoken subtext from our
teachers was that he was remedial and needed help. As a result,
he nicknamed me "Cleo-fatra" (Which in my opinion was a
rather clever play on words for a kid who wasn't being taught
properly and who teachers often dismissed as "trouble" in the
most problematic ways). Many days E would lead the rounds
of taunts but I soon learned a comeback that cut like a knife. I
could see it was sharp in the way his face fell and his eyes got
distant and far away. For every "Cleo-fatra" I would simply give
him my best withering look and say with disdain, "Can't you
READ?" It soon became my secret weapon of cruelty in a way
that only children can do. I was learning to make my own rules
now.

But that day on the playground, E saw us huddled together
in our winter coats, working intently in our notebooks long

after the recess bell had rung. This seemed to enrage him, and he lashed out at me with his hands for the first time instead of just his sharp tongue. He pulled the sleeves of my coat, and something within me shattered. I was suddenly tired. Tired of the names, and the social anxiety, and the "girl you think you're a white girl," and the "why do you talk like that to your Black friends?" and "Cleo-fatra," and the lack of chocolate milk.

I am embarrassed to say now that on that day I wished E would leave school and never come back to call me "Cleo-fatra" again. He was emphatically *not my nigga*. So when this boy twice my size reached for the sleeve of my coat, trying to use either side to drag me down, I quickly used all my strength to wriggle free of his hold. I sprung myself out of the coat one arm at a time, leaving him now with a powerful weapon to lash at my arms and face and chest and neck. As the zippered ends of the coat rained down on me like vicious fire, I did the only thing I could think to do: I hit him in the face. Gripping firmly the handle of my metal lunchbox, I hit him again and again and again and again and again. I hit him with all the force in my tiny body while he alternated between laughs of derision meant to tell me it didn't hurt and groans of pain that told me it did. I hit him while lunch monitors and children alike stood by and watched. After several minutes of beating, a lunch monitor intervened and gently asked me for my name. E went to the principal's office. I went back to lunch. The rules of a different game.

I never saw E after we left elementary school. I can't claim to think about him much.

* * *

When I was eighteen, I was riding in the car with one of my friends when another driver cut her off in traffic. We were singing some sort of boy band music and feeling the cool air blowing through the AC. It felt like a perfect day, or as close to perfect as days got when you were eighteen and driving slowly around suburbia. Suddenly, another driver came into our lane. The other driver was moving recklessly, scaring us both. She turned to him sharply, almost without thinking and said, "No you don't nigger!" before cutting the driver off. Both she and the other driver were white. We sat in silence after she said it, her face turned red while mine lost color. She apologized profusely. To me, to the other driver who couldn't possibly hear her, to the air. I laughed uncomfortably. I told her she didn't have to apologize, even though this was a lie, and I was stunned. It wounded me again to hear my tentative voice offering *her* platitudes as if I was the cause of some grave injury.

I had never heard this word used like a condemnation before. I had never heard it wielded in an anger with the intention to hurt or make someone smaller. To make them feel small and smaller still, until they were simply nothing but an empty void. I had only ever used it to mean kin, family, friend, fellow traveler. This was different.

I wanted to foolishly remember it only as a childhood secret shared in the farthest darkest corner of the cubby room. I wanted to remember a little boy who lifted me up off the blacktop and helped me to stand while inspecting my bloody hands. I wanted to remember my Black friends who said it with a sort of knowing tenderness, a signifier that we were interconnected. I wanted things that contradicted themselves and made little sense to me then and even less sense to me now.

I did not want the mishmash of memories from my childhood. I wanted the clear-cut delineations of right and wrong. Instead, we continued to ride in the car in complete silence, eating fast food burgers and watching TV together before she drove me home. I remember the worker in the drive-through got our order wrong that day, but it didn't matter. The food tasted dry and flavorless as I swallowed it, still thinking about that moment in the car. My eyes were vacant and glassy as I watched senseless TV for hours, quietly sitting in a house I had spent years of my life in at that point. I felt uneasy. Was nigger in the mouth of her parents who loved me and spoiled me and gave me special foods I liked whenever I came over? Was nigger at their dinner table when I wasn't around? Was it living and breathing in the heart of this friend who professed to know me intimately? It had to come from somewhere. To this day, I still don't know where. Maybe it came from deep within the recesses of an American heart: a thought, a feeling, a word that burns on the tip of their tongues, just waiting for the right moment to slip out past their teeth and lips. It certainly didn't come from nowhere, despite the randomness of the moment. It has to live somewhere. I do not want to live there, too, even though I do.

* * *

"It's like the worst feeling in the world. It just kind of pierces your heart." In college, a Black friend of mine from the Deep South is trying to describe to me what it feels like when a white person calls you a nigger.

By the time he says it, I don't need him to tell me anymore.

Dandelion

"Tallawah: 1. Strong, sturdy, not to be underestimated; tough; stubborn."

—*Dictionary of Jamaican English*

She is me.

She is still in mourning for a self that never was. A whole self, a milk and honey self, force ripe with the sweetness of lived girlhood. "You're an old soul," a friend of her mother whispers into the hollow of her ear, filling her head with a wet and longing sound. She still wonders what an old soul is. She does not and did not want an old soul. She wants and wanted to be new and shining, glistening, burnished, polished and resplendent, made that way by the steady movements of sure and loving hands.

An "old soul" always implied to her something that has aged before its time. It was likely her old soul that made her kindergarten teacher tell her mother that "Danielle is the saddest child I've ever seen," as if such a thing could be measured and quantified. An old soul that drew her closer to the world of adults at too young an age. Or maybe an old soul is a code for moody children with sharp tongues and observing eyes?

She lost her faith in the Church in her early teens, but still she regularly bows her head and clasps her hands fervently to make prayerful appeals to unseen deities. She still believes in the unspoken divine organization of the universe. These are hard habits to break, learned from summers spent in Black Pentecostal church camps deep in the woods. Early in the morning when the air was new and cold (and before breakfast was served) the children at camp would march in lines down to the wood-hewn chapel. Weak from hunger and lingering sleep they prayed. There, adults enveloped in the love, and sweat, and blood, and righteousness of their Christ would perform a laying on of hands. In Black English and spiritual practice to "lay hands" on someone can be in either violence or prayer.

In that chapel she had many damp palms pressed with passion-filled earnestness to her forehead. She learned the meaning of the word "willful" as it rained down on her stooped shoulders, half-peeking eyes, and upturned hands cupping air that was empty of substance but leaden with spirit. An old soul and a willful child. She waited for the goodness of God to roll through her. She wanted to feel the Holy Spirit move inside of her, shifting her sinful thoughts and failures. She wished God's grace would rain down on her. It never seemed to sweep her up in the nearly epileptic fits of majestic groaning and undulation that overtook the other children and adults. She wondered what she had done to displease God.

But still, she prayed. Today she prays.

In her childhood, her auntie and father dubbed her "Dandelion." When her siblings would tease her that those were the same weeds that their father routinely pulled out of the yard, he would quickly remind her that things could have a dual purpose. That they can be both a beautiful flower and a steadfast weed. She carries this truth with her through the years of her life.

By her adolescence, she longed for less duality, for a way to be legible. To be simple. To have a servant's heart. The men standing at the pulpit swore this was the way to be good, and she so wanted goodness. But it seemed the willful treachery of living life as a curious Black girl child had laid siege to her heart, and soon she learned to welcome it in. It was the same curiosity that pulled tight like a string on her sternum, directing her desires. She found her younger self often at the crossroads of these same desires, running like the river with the devil hot on her heels.

By the time she is thirteen, she is in the psychiatric emergency room with self-inflicted wounds and new scars running crisscross on her body. The lines trace the circuits of her wrists, arms, and thighs. The shame runs deeper than the shallow cuts and scabs. She hears her mother say to the doctors, "This isn't my daughter," and she wonders to herself, "Whose daughter am I then?" But she doesn't speak the words, knowing on some level that she is being difficult because she is scared.

What does it mean to be thirteen and to hate yourself? So much static rolling around a young mind warped by the bitter taste of self-loathing. She hates who she is right down to the root. She needs only so much vital energy and water and air. She convinces herself that one day soon she will die and turn into waste and be folded back into the red dirt, becoming fertilizer for the roots of beautiful trees that resemble her scars.

And yet she blooms. Still, she blooms.

She returns to the emergency room again at eighteen. New to college and drinking, she got so drunk she blacked out and wailed that she wanted to die again. When she wakes up she is strapped down to the bed, her hand covered in blood from when she tried to pull out her IV the night before (or so the doctor tells her). She cannot remember. She is more than a little surprised when they tell her why she's there. She believed she had left that all behind at thirteen when her parents and the school counselor made her see a therapist for two years. In the ER at eighteen there is a note from the friend who brought her here. It is folded into a large plastic bag with her clothes and other personal belongings. The note says he loves her and to call him when she wakes up. But all she can do is ask a nurse to take her to the bathroom on unsteady legs so that she can pee. After she is discharged she stands outside in the morning air under a sun she has no memory of seeing rise. She inhales the dew, checks her phone, and wonders, "Well, now what?"

She won't go back to the psych emergency room until she is twenty-four years old. In those six years between visits, she is afraid of herself and her mind. She learns to live alongside the sometimes-sudden sadness she calls "Blah Days." She calls her undiagnosed manic episodes "inspiration" and works past exhaustion, sometimes staying awake for forty-eight hours at a time. Some days she is glued to the bed and ignores knocks at the door, lying to say she is in "writer's isolation." Other times she drinks and dances and parties and laughs until she is nearly sick with feeling. She doesn't know then that these are all signs of dysregulation.

And yet she always grew. She grows.

At twenty-four years old, she returns from her first 72-hour hold in the psych ward. Maybe it is days after her return, or maybe months. The fluidity of dates and times from that period in her life makes her shudder when she remembers. She is still trying to make sense of that time, of herself, in relation to the slippage of those days, months, and years. On one of those days, the flowers on her nightstand wither and die, made dry by loving touches and over-fondling. These are the flowers she was given by a friend. She crushes their petal-softness in the flat of her hand, cherishing them with piercing love, as she releases their decaying sweetness back into essential air. She wonders to herself if dying is like the scent of the flowers: a thing that lingers to remind you of what used to be and yet still is. She struggles with thoughts of suicide during those days after the hospital, only deciding through stubbornness that she will not go that easily. Instead, she tattoos *Tallawah* on the wrist of her writing hand.

All around her in these years she sees evidence of the precarity of Black life. She sees surveillance and cellphone videos, grainy in the darkness or sometimes painfully clear, of Black/brown bodies being murdered on the news. Demanding only so much air, so much breath. Or washed-up face down and lifeless on the beach or some city street, dead for hours, devoid of attentive loving touch. What would she ask God for on her knees? For them? For her formerly suicidal self? For herself in the wake of them? For herself alone? She longs for space, to take up space, to exist somewhere outside of a world that seems so determined to age Black/brown souls. To make us small and smaller still, until we are only so much dust, disintegrated in spite or because of loving fondling. She cannot watch the images anymore. Cannot justify how they bring about her own terror-tinged sadness and rage. And yet both feelings are just.

Twenty-six. She sees the people of Baltimore rising up in the streets after the 2016 murder of Freddie Gray at the hands of the police. A well-coiffed white woman stands in the emptiness of a looted drug store on TV and reports on what the protestors have taken. The woman is surrounded by rows and rows of empty shelves and broken glass. She comes to full attention when the reporter on TV notes that protestors have taken a whole store's worth of Abilify, the name for the same antipsychotic drug doctors have been pumping her full of since she was twenty-four. As far as she knows it can't be used to get high, giving it very little street value. But it can be used to treat depression, bipolar depression, and schizophrenia. She is still three years and one more hospitalization away from a diagnosis of bipolar depression. So she guesses this is a different kind of feel-good drug. Black/brown bodies on the news and in the streets, rising up and trying to feel good, whole, and sane.

She stares at the screen, at the empty shelves that used to be filled with neatly labeled pills. What is the name for the illness that wraps itself around the minds of Black/brown people until we are choking on our own necessary ingestion of air? What is the cure for a world so dead set on our madness?

She remembers on that night that she was watching the news out of Baltimore that the church people of her Pentecostal upbringing believe that they can cure what ails the body through a laying on of hands. The kind of laying on of hands that is meant to heal and not harm. She wonders when she will be schooled in appropriate mourning. How can she hold the collective sadness of Black/brown life in the same hands that cupped spirit air and clasped fervently together to beg the Lord for his mercy? How to reconcile the praying daughter and the old soul of the willful child?

She misses the sun in her mind. The same sun that nourishes both the petal-softness of the flower and the bark-clad body of the tree.

And so, she prays:

Make in me a bounty. Carry me through the valleys and on the hilltops. Make of my life an offering of goodness. Make of me a compassionate conqueror. Make the spirit of the divine resonate from the center of my life. Let it order my steps. Make me strong in self-protection, in protection, in love.

The flowers on my nightstand have died, made dry from too much loving fondling. And on my final day, make me like the wither of the flower.

On Love Songs

I knew as soon as I heard my first note that I loved love songs. I loved those songs the way some people love science fiction. You don't have to go to space to marvel at the vastness of the universe. I didn't have to fall in love to wonder at the depths of human emotion, cruelty, stupidity, and contradiction. To me, a love like that was like another planet. I'd just listen to those lyrics and groove away into space.

As a child, I was a devotee of Aretha Franklin's anthem "Call Me." My mother owned a compilation CD that we would play in the car on special days, and I would tentatively sing Ms. Franklin's opening lyrics, a conversation between two lovers saying simple "I love yous" and promising to "Call me the moment you get there." These simple declarations comprised my first fantasies of what it would mean to have a lover: someone waiting patiently by the phone line just to whisper one more "I love you" through the connection. I loved this compilation CD with its red cover and silhouette picture of Aretha on the front. I loved "Do Right Woman, Do Right Man," a reminder to all those faithless lovers that if you wanted a woman to treat you well in public, then you'd better make damn sure you loved her well in private. I loved "Chain of Fools" and all the other tracks on the CD. But "Call Me" was a standout. At that age, I was loved and loved well by many of the adults in my life. Mom, Dad, aunties, uncles, cousins, and other kinfolk showed me through actions more than words that I was cherished. And yet I wanted that whispered, plaintive "I love you" to echo down the phone line. I wanted someone to love me who I felt didn't "have to" in the way my family did. On reflection, I was quite a romantic child, even though as a pansexual/bisexual person who knew this about myself from age thirteen onwards, I never really fantasized about my wedding day or what my partner would look like. That void used to trouble me as a teenager, but I grew to accept it in adulthood. Because I couldn't envision anything of this in my head, I accepted that I wouldn't partner and would never marry, instead contenting myself with fleeting and frivolous connections in my twenties.

I was never blessed with an ear for playing musical instruments, but even so, I liked to sing. As a child, I would often lock myself in my bedroom closet with a little handheld tape recorder, the shoes on the floor digging into my backside, and sing quietly into the speaker. Songs about giving "My All" by Mariah Carey, or being "All The Man That I Need" by Whitney, or Ms. Lauryn Hill's version of "Can't Take My Eyes Off You." When I was really feeling myself, I'd switch it up with a defiant Tina wailing in the most beautiful rasp, "What's Love Got to Do with It?" or Chaka Khan deeply belting for her lover to "Tell Me Something Good." Even back then, with the plastic bows in my hair keeping time, I knew that love had a lot to do with it. Maybe everything. I knew that it was the "something good" Chaka demanded. I wanted to reach high notes like Whitney with all of the passion and power that caused her to be dubbed "The Voice." From an early age, I had a deeper-than-average voice for a girl child, so I knew Mariah's whistle notes would remain in the realm of fantasy for me. My light alto voice could never match the soaring sopranos of the Black women I admired at that age, but I still made my tapes and listened to them eagerly, with the small speaker pressed against my ear. It didn't sound like Tina's rasp or Chaka's rock and roll, but it still sounded good enough to make me peel back my lips in a little smile that showed off all of my baby teeth. I wanted to know those grown woman blues that made them beckon their menfolk to their bedsides. I wanted to know the secrets of swinging hips and undulating vocals, and strong struts in music videos and on award show stages.

And just as religiously as I recorded these secret songs, I recorded over every note as soon as I was done. I was too embarrassed to admit what I had done: what I longed for while sitting on the shoes in the closet. Instead, I hid my desire behind shame and womanish sass. I found the recorder in my childhood bedroom recently, the same tape inside waiting for the notes of my voice whispering into the microphone. Its pink and purple plastic body strikes me as extremely garish now, even though in childhood it had seemed perfect in my eyes. Now the plastic looks cartoonish and bright. I wonder if there is anything on the tape still inside, but a lack of AA batteries prevents me from finding out.

Despite my dedication to the swoony ballads and soaring solos of my childhood, I grew up into a rather romantically avoidant adult. I spent my twenties in blazing defiance against love. My life was seemingly full of it (friendships, family, colleagues), and yet the one love people write the most songs about continuously eluded me. I went on dates, had fun, had sex, got drunk, and danced so hard on so many dance floors I felt like I would break or fall apart. I studied, got my degrees, got a job, and continued to fuck, dance, and laugh my way through and away from romance. I opened many incognito browsers to google things like "Why can't I fall in love?" and "Am I aromantic?" I laughed it off and continued onwards, but these questions continued to plague me. I don't regret the romantic voids of my twenties, in part because those years happened to coincide with the period of my greatest psychiatric dysregulation, marking some of the scariest moments of my young life. Although more incognito googling on bipolar depression after my diagnosis at twenty-nine revealed that, while in some ways the development of my illness was quite textbook and average for people with this disease, I experienced my worsening symptoms as a series of painful surprises. I didn't know which days would be "good" and which days would be lost to anxiety, paranoia, mania, depression, or some combination of all of these things. It didn't matter that later, I discovered this was pretty normal for people with bipolar depression who were not on the right meds. It didn't matter that most people with bipolar depression experience the onset of acute symptoms in their early twenties (just like I did). All of this I discovered in hindsight, and so without a clear path ahead of me, I deemed myself "too difficult" to date. After I decided this in my early twenties, I made up my mind about two supposed facts about me:

1) I was "too difficult" and moody to fall in love with.

2) Someone as "difficult" as me was better off alone or only having brief, casual, and fleeting primarily sexual affairs.

By the time I returned from my first 72-hour psych hold at the ripe old age of twenty-four, I had written off the love I longed for as a child completely. I would instead be a difficult woman. In my heart, I harbored a secret disdain for people who fell in love too quickly. I condescendingly pitied them for their naivete and their dedication to heartache. I said to myself in my most superior tone, "I would NEVER marry/love/give my heart to the first person who asked." Not that anyone in particular was asking. I just considered myself too smart and achingly lonely for all of that. I laughed and laughed and cried and laughed. And I continued to wonder in some small corner of my heart if I was just irreparably broken.

I think it's important to mention here that I had a happy childhood. I had siblings and friends, parents, aunties, uncles, cousins, love. I grew up in a house with more bedrooms than people and with more food than hunger and more joy than anger. I was given a good sense of myself in the world from an early age. I had a firm belief that one day I would be a person with my name on the spine of a book from age seven until today. I still write like I am trying to save a life and that the life that I am trying to save is my own. I am trying to save it from extinction, from anonymity, from precarity, from peril. I am trying to save it up like new money or something else that's shiny and unspeakably precious. I am trying to save it for and from myself. For a rainy day when I may need more life. From a mind and body that feel hell-bent on eating themselves alive. For Black blue girls who want to love and be loved in the most ferocious way, a way that I never truly believed was possible for me when I was sitting on my shoes in the closet recording songs. I write about myself mostly for these reasons. And yet for all my furious writing for and because of life, I've always secretly hoped to write a love song that soars people to the heights of emotion that one lyric can do. If I could write one song like that, I'd give up my dream of seeing my name on the spine of a book, a dream that's defined me since I was seven years old.

"I don't think we should cannibalize other people's stories to tell our own."

I am twenty-six. I say this in the fancy, exclusive writer's workshop class that I almost drove myself half-/full-crazy to get into. (The fancy, exclusive writer's workshop where the other mostly white writers in my class make it very clear they do not like my work.) I immediately become enchanted with this sentence and the way it sounds and so I say it again in another context when someone asks me about writing a memoir. Because I worry as I write that I will hurt the people who have loved me well. Not the mostly anonymous lovers of my twenties, or the half-forgotten one-off dates of my early thirties. Not the people with whom I shared so much of my body and so little of my spirit. But the friends, and family, and friends' friends, and colleagues who loved me into life. Whose consistency gave structure to my days and my darkest nights. But despite being well-loved, I've also always felt the gnawing hunger for that good love, that belting soprano love, that "write a love song that makes you ache with feeling" love. At twenty-six I was creative, insecure, and the kind of self-righteous that can only be born out of being creative and insecure. Even now as I write about this hunger, I worry that I will wound the people who have loved me and loved me well. Why can't that be enough? And still, I write it all down, call it back to myself, draft it into being.

Every day.

I can't write when I listen to music. It gets me too confused. When I listen, I close my eyes to fall even deeper into the sounds until I don't know where I end and the singer begins. I write in silence so that I can reliably know the only voice I'm hearing is my own. But I grow tired of singing solos and long for the sweet, mellow harmonies of a duet.

I am in the shower when my lover hears me singing. I am thirty-one years old. Ms. Lauryn Hill is on the playlist today. When I emerge, all Black-brown, soft, and dewy from the steam, they kiss my face and tell me they like to hear me sing. That I have a pretty voice. And I melt into the shower rug, deep into the folds of the small square of waterproof carpet that I am never quite sure how to clean. Do you put it in the washer? The dryer? Hand-wash it?

This is a lover who changed my belief in love. I want to sing a million love-stung anthems at their feet, ladle down praise on them like hot syrup on waffles (even though that image makes me laugh and laugh and cry and laugh). They shifted the insides of me, made me feel less irreparably broken. Taught me the meaning of the notes I'd long admired but never truly reconciled in my head. Made me shed the shame for loving that drove me into the farthest corners of my childhood closet, erasing tape after tape on my little recorder. This is the first person I've ever called lover without a hint of sarcasm in the word. The first person who has claimed the term "partner" from me. The first person I felt made me part of a pair.

The first time they told me they loved me I was in crisis. Family disaster weighed heavily on my spirit and my lover was supposed to have dinner at my place that night. I was feeling the pulse of my own sadness in the center of my forehead and my limbs felt weak and leaden with grief from a family story that is not mine to tell. Not here. I was cooking something new and vegetarian (My lover was new and vegetarian, even though I am dedicatedly carnivorous.) I told them on the phone what ailed my spirit, and they said, "I don't have to come over tonight." But I wanted the company and told them so. They arrived with a bouquet and ice cream, which I accepted eagerly but did not comment on. I have always felt most things acutely. I do not know if it is more or less than other folks, but the sharp sting of my emotions has chased me my whole life. A week before this dinner I had told a friend that I was in love with my lover, but I was only "chest-deep in love. It's not like I'm up to my eyeballs in it yet!" My friend and I laughed at the metaphor and laughed and laughed and he said, "Good. I'm happy for you." On the night in question, I stood over the stove silently shedding tears about familial pain, and stirring the vegetarian food in the pot. I felt two strong hands on my waist from behind gently rubbing the folds in my back and sides that I've been taught to despise, but that they profess to love. I felt the two hands circle around to my rounded stomach and I felt it roll over in anxiety and unnamed emotion. I had taken to listening to Sam Smith's ballad "Say It First" about an anxious lover who doesn't know how to say "I love you" in the weeks leading up to this moment. The song is slow and steady, without too many high points or fancy flourishes. Smith's entreaties to an unnamed lover go unanswered. I am nothing if not literal. I felt my lover's mouth sharing a warm breath in the shell of my ear. I felt it before I heard the words. "I love you," they said. And as many times as I've heard the words before from family, friends, colleagues, strangers, acquaintances, and others, it was the first time I heard them in romance. And just like that, I was up to my eyeballs in it, feeling the feelings of Mariah, Whitney, Tina, and Chaka. I said it back, all at once and in a rush, scared it wouldn't be repeated. "I love you too."

These words felt like swallowing dry toast on my tongue: nourishing and somewhat choking. I said it again, this time without the "too." Just plain. "I love you." It was a revelation to me in that moment that I was even capable of these emotions, let alone expressing them so freely.

In that moment I heard Ms. Lauryn Hill's entreaty to "Turn Your Lights Down Low." I heard music that moved my seven-year-old Black-and-blue girl heart to tears. I heard sweetness and song. I wanted crescendos and whistle notes and hooks and sappy choruses. I wanted the language to explain all of this to someone (Although it's never quite as fun to explain a song as it is to sing one.) All of those adolescent fantasies I'd repressed in the years when I was dancing, and fucking, and running from loving came rushing back all at once in the sharpest relief.

Their love felt like a yielding place.

That night in bed we were moving over and under and through each other. I said it first that time because I wanted to know that it was real, that it really had happened the way I thought it did, the way I remembered it. I wanted to soar and shape myself around and against this feeling forever. For all my lofty talk in the writing workshop, I wanted to consume them, to eat their love alive and let it expand my empty round belly they profess to love the curves of. I want to cannibalize this fleshy feeling and swallow it whole. I feel this feeling most folks experience in their teens for the first time in my thirties and wonder if I'm too old to be this dramatic. I wish I had a belting soprano and a craft for writing songs so I can sing it out to my lover in the most dramatic overtones. Sing it high and loud and strong until we are both caught up in the rapture.

I want to sing our way into space.

Numbers

He was definitely going to die.

I mean, he was up there. I mean WAY up there, so many feet above the blue mats that there was no way his nine-year-old body could survive the fall. The children in gym class stood in a semicircle around the swinging tail end of the rope, watching him place hand over fist and squirm his entwined legs. Even the gym teacher watched with a certain amount of amazement. It wasn't just that he was going farther than any other child in gym class had gone before (Little strips of blue tape noted the quarter, halfway, and three-quarter marks of the climbing rope.) It wasn't only that the only other child (a boy with pale skin and hazel-colored freckles) to make it to the top of a rope had done so on the rope with the big fat knots in it that you could climb like a ladder to make it easier.

It was his speed. He was moving faster than I thought was even possible to get up the ropes. He was so determined, using his hands to pull his fighting abdomen and tightly wrapped legs. My mouth fell open as he got to the top of the rope where it connected with the rafters of the ceiling. Being a short, bookish, fat, and uncoordinated Black girl who was afraid of heights, I had never made it past the quarter mark myself. And even then, that was on the "easy" rope with the big fat knots. I would climb halfway and then hang there in terror until the gym teacher took pity and let me slide back down.

I didn't like ropes that much. Neither climbing them, nor jumping through them was much fun. Especially when you didn't have the strength necessary for the former, or the rhythm needed for the latter. My best friend at the time was a light-skinned Haitian girl with big Shirley Temple curls and attitude. She always convinced me to try to learn Double Dutch. Every time the ropes came out in gym class or on the blacktop, she would try to give what she thought were helpful instructions: "You just have to count it. Jump in … now. Now. Jump in NOW!" I got too embarrassed after a certain point to keep trying in front of the other girls. Tired of freeing myself from the tangles or getting whiplashed in the face by the fast-moving ropes. So, I learned to turn the ropes instead. I was proud of this, because after a while other girls thought I was one of the better rope turners and whenever Double Dutch was happening, I always had a guaranteed spot. Plus, I wasn't what they called "double-handed" and didn't lose the beat or let the ropes kiss and tangle as often as the other jump rope turners did. Most Black girls wanted to jump anyway, so being a turner for an hour guaranteed my place near the flock with a built-in excuse to always skip my chance to jump.

Plus, I memorized the words to all the rhymes and knew how to whip those ropes so fast they almost looked like a translucent force field surrounding the bodies in the center with their Black brown legs beating hard steps against the ground.

My head hurt / My bra too tight / My booty shaking from left to right / Left to right / Left left, to right / Left to right, left left to right.

Teddy bear teddy bear turn around / Teddy bear teddy bear touch the ground.

Down down baby / Down down the rollercoaster / Sweet sweet baby / I'll never let you go / Shimmy shimmy cocoa pop / Shimmy Shimmy pow / Shimmy shimmy cocoa pop / Shimmy shimmy pow.

We're number one / not number two / We're gonna kick the (____) outta you!

But today this boy was going to make it to the top. He was already most of the way there. His dark skin looked like mine, but his body was decidedly wiry and thin. We were about the same height and sometimes got paired together in class in a weird "buddy system" the teacher enforced. I was supposed to help him with his classwork, but mostly it seemed like the teacher wanted me to keep him quiet. I was a "good girl": bookish and timid and likely to do anything I was told by a teacher. He was "bad" because he didn't like to finish his worksheets and often went to detention. As I got older, I realized how oversimplified this was, and resented in retrospect my teachers making me do this task.

As the class started chanting and he finally reached the apex of the ropes, an enormous cheer broke out. Even our usually solemn gym teacher cracked a tentative smile. He looked down on us with his straight face and squinted eyes, smiling broadly. He even managed to take one hand off the rope and pump it twice in the air. Then the cheering turned to silence and a collective gasp as he reached his free hand over to the ceiling rafters and made a move like he was going to climb off of the ropes and slide along the bar. The students screamed, and the gym teacher's temporary smile melted as she blew her sharp silver whistle and commanded that he come down to the blue mats. Until he got there, she seemed more terrified than angry. Once he landed, her hand was firmly on his elbow, and she was hauling him into the little office designated for the gym teachers. Everyone liked those other teachers better than her anyway. The "free time" box of gym equipment (jump ropes, dodge balls, tennis racquets) was brought out. Everyone else got a free period while the gym teacher eventually marched him down to the principal's office. Even though we were glad for the free time, we didn't stop tittering about the brave boy's climb and his hand poised above the rope reaching for the ceiling rafters.

And we all agreed with a solemn consensus: he definitely would have died.

During this free period, I took up my usual position at the ends of the Double Dutch ropes and wondered. I didn't like him much. I didn't like being his buddy in class, or the way he never listened to teachers or the way he called me names when I sat around the playground reading books or making up poems with my friends. I didn't like that sometime over the previous summer he had learned some crude things about sex that neither of us really understood, but he would say them to me sometimes just to make me mad. I didn't like how he would grab his crotch and shake it in my direction when I told him he was stupid. I didn't care that he could climb the ropes, that he was faster than all the other boys in the class despite his small size. But the moment when he reached for the ceiling rafter, I thought for just a second that he was kind of cute. But it dissipated as soon as the gym teacher yelled at him to come down.

Years later when I am eighteen and voting for the first time I will return to my elementary school because it is my polling place. Wandering through the halls to the gym where the voting stations are, I marvel at how small everything looks to me now. The whole building seems like a dollhouse, with short little desks and chairs. The bulletin boards are all at least a foot lower than anywhere else (presumably to catch children at their eye level). Even the toilets are six inches to a foot closer to the ground. The only thing that seems to be the same size is the height of the gym ceiling. I look up and see the ropes where they are still knotted against the wall on one end and hanging from the ceiling on the other. The rafters are at least twelve to fifteen feet away from the floor. I still maintain: if he hadn't died, he would have at least been seriously hurt. A body so small couldn't have sustained a fall that far without consequences.

For years I remember this boy on the ropes as the one who forcibly gave me my first kiss. I remember him walking over as he passed me in the gym around third grade, leaning over to press his chapped lips to mine before walking calmly to his spot on the mat as if nothing had happened. It was a rare moment when the gym teacher's back was to us, or she was in her office, or simply not paying attention. Theatrically, I used the back of my hand to wipe my mouth, indicating my disgust for him. He merely smiled. In my twenties I flip through a yearbook and see his picture. I also see a picture of another boy with a different name and all of a sudden, I remember it was him who kissed me, not the boy from the ropes. Out of curiosity I google the rope climber's name and discover that he had been murdered in our early twenties. Police believe he was attempting to steal a car with his friend when the owner returned and shot them both. The stories I find online in 2014 are sparse and contain very little detail. What an insufficient way to sum up a life. I'd rather remember him climbing.

* * *

I am bad at math, but I am good at numbers.

Lining the blacktop in pairs are little Black girls with their hair in braids and bows. We are learning the logic of the game against the rhythm of our bodies. Clap hands on one, slap hands on two, flip hands around on three, slap thighs on four. This is a game we call "Numbers." Numbers isn't played in time to a tune or a rhyme. Instead, your body becomes the percussive instrument, keeping the time, driving the beat until sore hands or exhaustion call an end to the game.

I am pretty good at Numbers. The repetitions of the movements and the predictability of the clapping mean that I can focus on the thing that I love most: speed. I always drive the tempo slightly faster in each round, pushing my opponent to keep up with me or perish. I will continue on even after my hands are sore and my wrists are numb. I push faster and faster, keeping time in my head until one of us trips up and the game falls apart.

13, 18, 24, 29. I have been to the psychiatric emergency room 4 times in my life. 5 years, 6 years, 5 years. The intervals between each visit have remained shockingly consistent. Now I measure my wellness in numbers. 1 therapy session a week. 6 months until my next psychiatry appointment. 5 pills a day (a cocktail of prescriptions and vitamins).

13, 18, 24, 29.

5, 6, 5.

1, 6, 5.

I go over the numbers of illness every day, trying to find a pattern. The randomness of life opens up before me like a giant gaping maw. But patterns are safe. Patterns will keep me safe. If I continue to turn the numbers over in my hands and in my head, I will crack the code, cheat the game, and win the prize. If I find a reason for all of this, I will finally decipher a meaning, and if I have a meaning then maybe I will be whole.

13- self-mutilation, suicidal ideation.

18- suspected alcohol poisoning and suicidality.

24- psychotic break and mania.

29- psychotic break and mania.

5 years: between the end of middle school and the beginning of college.

6 years: weeks before my oral exams in grad school.

5 years: the end of my first year as a postdoc.

Daily pills.

Weekly appointments.

Monthly check-ins.

Twenty-nine years old, after years of being told that my diagnosis was "stress," "depression," and "anxiety," I am diagnosed with bipolar depression 1. Twenty-nine before I hear those words in relation to myself. I savor the diagnosis like sour candy or raw onion, something that at once delights and tortures the taste buds. I pucker my mouth around it and say it often. Bipolar depression 1. Suddenly there appears to be a pattern where once there were only scatters of data. With a diagnosis comes late nights of googling answers. "What is bipolar depression?" "How to know if you have bipolar depression?" "Bipolar depression treatment?" "Bipolar depression cure?"

I become an autodidact of my own health. I digest what I learn and try to learn more.

* * *

I am definitely going to die. It likely won't be now and it likely won't be today, but this immutable fact remains the only constant of living.

When I do, I will be added to the countless number of people who have faced death before, whether I am ready or not.

In college, I took a lecture on Introduction to Statistics. I wasn't particularly good at it, but I loved the logic of the math. It felt more practical than the things we'd had to tackle in high school (algebra, geometry, and calculus) and so I gravitated toward it. I remember one day jotting down notes about "question bias" and why we shouldn't trust self-reported online reviews because they generally represent the extremes of customer satisfaction and dissatisfaction. Our lecturer said the only reason someone writes a review is because they are overly satisfied or extremely dissatisfied.

After that I become obsessed with statistics, whether they relate to me or not. Of particular interest are the statistics around Black women and bipolar depression. Although I remained undiagnosed and/or misdiagnosed for sixteen years, I am also interested in the numbers of Black women who are improperly diagnosed with this disease. Diagnosis felt so rational when it happened to me because I was eager for information and to not "become a statistic" as the old adage goes. I looked for reasons where there seemed to be none (or at least very little). I read broadly and indiscriminately about trauma and childhood and genetics and inheritance, searching for an answer wrapped within a question. I am determined to enliven my story, to divorce it from the numbers, even as I am indelibly tied to other Black women like me who have suffered and continue to suffer. I read in an article online that Black people are more likely to experience psychosis than their white counterparts. The author doesn't offer any definitive explanation for this fact, which leaves me dissatisfied and curious.

I want something orderly and neat. I want to straighten the record until it cannot yield. I want reason in the wake of emotion, as if those two feelings aren't twins.

* * *

When I was school aged, I loved plain white milk.

Like most public schools in the US, my elementary school gave away milk with every meal. Breakfast, snack time, lunch, after school, field trips. Everyone got a container of subsidized milk.

Although I didn't qualify to get all of my meals from the school like many of my classmates, I still bought lunch several days a week and attended the after-school programs. But because I was a fat and gluttonous child, I was often hungry.

By the time I was in first or second grade I figured out a key fact: if you requested chocolate or strawberry milk you could only have one. But if you asked for plain milk in the blue cartons, you could have as many as you wanted. The flavored milks were popular and heavily rationed. But the school received an equal amount, if not more, of the plain white stuff. From the day I first timidly asked the lunch attendant if I could take two cartons and she responded by dropping three on my tray, I became hooked on white milk.

I drank it all the time: at school, at my own home, at the homes of my friends, in Girl Scout troop meetings, during snack time. By the time I went to Catholic school I had grown accustomed to drinking milk on my own and started buying it by choice. In college, milk was still subsidized by the state. The cafeteria had a drink dispenser that was dedicated entirely to milk. Once or twice a day I'd drink a glass from the huge vats or siphon some off in disposable coffee cups to take home. Milk was always there; it was always available. I associated it with fullness and being favored, even in a small way, by the lunch ladies who came to tease me about my vociferous appetite for milk. I even laughed about how I'd drink milk and eat potato chips or Cheetos because it was essentially water to me.

By the time I turned twenty-two I didn't actively think about milk. It was just something I sat down to have every day. But because I was living on my own without access to cafeteria subsidized milk for the first time in my life, I unconsciously stopped drinking it for about four months during the summer after college graduation. One day as I was leaving my apartment for the week, I noticed I had a brand new pint of unopened milk in the fridge, about one week away from the sell-by date. Since I wasn't sure if I'd be back in time to finish it, I drank the carton quickly before I left home.

For the next thirty-six hours as I kept rushing to the toilet, groaning, with my insides stripping out of my ass, I realized for the first time that I can't digest milk. That, like most of the people in my family and many Black people, I am severely lactose intolerant. That I've been lactose intolerant my entire life. That my aversion to other dairy products that I wasn't conditioned to like, an aversion I always assumed had to do with not enjoying those foods rather than any kind of negative reaction to them, actually stemmed from my body rejecting dairy. My great exception was milk, which I consumed with the steady pace and dependency of an addict.

"How did I teach myself to love and willingly consume so much of something that makes me sick?" I wondered at the end of those early awareness days. Why did I act as if I needed milk to survive? How didn't I notice that milk was slowly fucking up my system, even in the early years when I had to see a doctor about my indigestion and constipation issues? No one was standing over me, making me drink it. In fact, after a certain point I trained myself to have it every day without prompting. I associated my acceptance of milk with good things: being healthy, being different or sturdier than my allergy-prone siblings, being an easy-going child, being helpful. I thought I was like a '50s *Leave it to Beaver* kid because I drank milk after school.

But I realized at twenty-two that milk was always making me sick. That it was always fucking me up. That I'd conditioned my mind to ignore the signs because I wanted to be a "milk person." I wanted to claim some of that goodness, that ideal, that insidious message of wholesome consumption, even the sexiness of the late '90s "Got Milk?" ads, for myself. I wanted to be that way.

So, I told myself I loved milk. I ignored any evidence to the contrary (genetics, medical advice, anecdotal observations). I did all this willfully and unconsciously for twenty-two years. I bent and changed my perception of myself until it fit the things I was subsidized to take.

When my mind trained itself to resist what my body knows, it became the most powerful tool in my own self-deception.

* * *

The boy on the ropes was not my friend. I didn't even like him much. Yet I feel compelled to write him a love note, to give flesh to the number that his life became. Maybe I am trying to breathe life into my own gaping mouth, to feed my own gnawing hunger for relevance.

Some stories and story-shaped lies are easy to tell and digest, simply because they have the air of truth about them. Like shooting fish in a barrel and calling it sport.

Or when I whisper to myself at night, "I only have so many heartbreaks left in me," with the contained agony I save for pillow whispers. But this assumes that there is a definitive hierarchy of hurt, where cuts are worse than bruises, and cracks are superior to cleaves. And I know this isn't true.

Sometimes I fear I'm just breaking along the routes of the same weakened lines, like my body is making itself more malleable in anticipation of absorbing future jolts. It all just savors of pain and for this above all else I have a great capacity.

The boy on the rope would grow to be a man who died too young. I am still at an age where if I died people would wail and proclaim it "too young." I never saw him again after we left the fifth grade.

I heard somewhere once that people who live in really densely populated areas rarely ever get the chance to scream. To let all the air out from their guts to the top of the chest. Screams in these areas are reserved for raising the alarm. They are not cathartic.

I haven't given voice to a full-body scream in many years.

The driver of the car who killed the boy from gym class was later arrested and charged with murder. I do not know how the story ends after that.

One day in my apartment in Connecticut, I texted my friend the story of the boy who climbed to the rafters. My friend jokes that he would "like to meet this gym class rock star!" It was on that day that I searched for his name online and discovered him dead. Now he has returned to dust, his body another number claimed by American violence. This is a violence with a seemingly insatiable appetite for Black suffering and death. I wonder if there is any question bias in the statistics. Will the numbers I count against my body maintain their percussive rhythm or simply fail and fall apart?

* * *

Stories culled from memories are more elemental than accurate. They are unreleased screams, swallowed back into the body before becoming reabsorbed. They are the bruised things, pulling skin from the roof of my mouth, tender to tell.

214

I Could Only Say Thank You
(Part 3)

By maybe the third or fourth week in town I finally grew accustomed to the overly affectionate way Italians have of touching. I've never been much of a hugger myself, but I enjoyed the warm hugs of my hostess and the way she framed my face in her cool hands, singing "Brava Dani!" while we dusted the rafters of our attic room. I smiled when our Italian and international opera stars pecked me casually on both cheeks every time I granted them special favors. I began to chirpily greet every old person out sunning themselves in the street, waving happily as I said "Boun giorno!" in my awful accent. Sometimes, older Italian women with weathered, kind faces would run their hands against the surface of my forearm as we spoke, and I wondered if they were testing my skin's texture or if this was just a universal habit. When they talked, the Italians I met often lurched forward, connecting their hands, fingers, forearms, or other parts of their bodies to the surfaces of mine. These friendly gestures made me feel a certain level of warmth towards this place.

However, I was still scared of the ripples of interest I had attracted among older white men. I stopped waving to them in the street when they sat next to their women. I noticed the Italian woman in her early sixties who owned the family bakery where I picked up my daily breakfast pastry glared at her husband every time I entered the store. He was paunchy and perhaps in his seventies with a nose that showed prolonged signs of alcohol consumption, his white skin mottled from years of chain smoking. He was old enough to be my grandfather. One day, he slipped me a small plastic bracelet, and another time, he gave our group a free bottle of wine, professing his love to me in Italian while someone in the group translated his words. The other people I was with looked on and smiled at me benevolently as if this was truly flattering. I turned on my heel and ran back towards the street. I have always been awkward around the attention of straight men, even those I have professed to like. Something about it makes me uneasy. I did not drink any of the free wine, but a perverse part of me felt compelled to shove the bracelet into my purse so I wouldn't offend him. A full twelve months later, I found the bracelet there in my purse, resting in the pocket hidden inside the lining. I cried bitterly at the memory of feeling like I couldn't just toss it, and strangely returned it to its place in the pocket. I will never use that purse again.

Another day, he grabbed me by my shoulders and presented my humiliated face to his son in his thirties like a prized pony. His son agreed in Italian that I was very beautiful as I contemplated the best way to struggle out of his arms without causing a scene. This man was gripping me and dragging me around, and yet I was afraid that I was the one causing a scene. After that, I asked my friends on the crew if we could frequent another bakery further down the street. They didn't seem to understand my request, and I felt ashamed afterward for even asking. I began to eat almost exclusively in the American café that used to play the loud Bob Marley music, and soon, the others complacently followed my lead, although sometimes they still insisted on holding full company meetings in the bakery's outdoor seating area. I began to only choose seats that were wedged with my back against the corner or in the very center of the couches with two people flanking me. I figured this made me less accessible to unwanted hands. I bowed my head to avoid the gazes of both father and son.

(_____) and I nicknamed the son "the German Strangler." This is because he was unusually tall (at least a good foot taller than most Italian men) and very noticeably blond and pale in a town filled primarily with jet-black hair and Mediterranean complexions. Another reason for the name arose from an incident that occurred around our third or fourth week in town, just as I was growing accustomed to the Italian way of touching. One day, I approached the counter, nodding a cautious acknowledgment to him from behind my overly large sunglasses. I asked warily for my usual morning pastry and a cappuccino. He said something jauntily in Italian, to which I offered my usual mumbled response, "Non capisco." I don't understand.

I tipped my head forward to inspect the confines of my purse, rooting around for the handful of euros I'd dropped in there earlier. As my hand reached into my purse, both of his arms came over the counter, and his large hands weaved their way into my hair. I froze, alarmingly aware of the vulnerability of my neck, with his hands bracketing my skull that way. I swallowed and stood still, panicking that if I jerked away suddenly, he would choose to hold on, even though his extremely calm and delighted demeanor didn't indicate any sort of conscious hostility. I stayed still as he measured my scalp and the shape of my head in his hands, the way someone would pet a breed of dog that they do not entirely recognize or trust. Perhaps it is fitting that it reminded me of being a dog because, in that moment, I felt dissociated and less than human. I felt like my body was an animal for him to inspect, regardless of my permission or consent. My hand remained frozen in my purse while he stayed in my hair. My eyes darted around, looking for assistance. He continued picking around my head for another ten seconds before finally withdrawing his hands. I thought in a panic that someone might say something to defend me. But (_____) was not there, and everyone whose eyes I met in the bakery was staring at me as if to say, "Well, what is it like?" Their curiosity seemed to outweigh any need to check in on my comfort.

I wondered if what he had said earlier had something to do with that, or if he was simply asking a question about my order. I guess I will never know. I exhaled slowly and threw my money down on the counter, hoping to make a hasty retreat. The clang from the change was still ringing in my ears as he laughed and said something else I couldn't understand. I did not have Italian words to explain to him why I didn't want him to do that. How it made me feel small and objectified and curious and less than human. I didn't even have English words. I wished at that moment that I had a gift for brilliant cutting comebacks and one-liners. But I remained trapped by the words that wouldn't come. I actually swallowed hard one more time, thanked him for the coffee, and scuttled away. From that day forward (_____) and I dub him "Strangler."

On the opening night of our show, the family that owned the bakery threw us a big dinner party. I chose the seat up against the wall with five people on either side of me. At one point, I was removed from the table and ushered over to stand between father and son to take a picture. Somewhere in that small town, there is a picture of me sandwiched between their massive shoulders, smiling to mask the mounting anxiety that is building in my throat and the backs of my hollowed-out eyes. I assumed at the time that the picture was one of the unspoken costs of this party since no one else was asked to stand. The camera clicked, the crowd cheered, and I returned to my seat. I felt my heartbeat in my temple as I sat down. Maybe I had gotten so used to the disregard for my feelings that I was effectively covering my dread. I learned to smile the way most women learn to smile in the face of unwanted male attention.

Late one night in a drunken stupor, a member of my company asked me bluntly, "Why do all of the men around here love you?!" I hesitated in my answer, uncomfortable with identifying my experience here as anything remotely related to love. I associated it more with being exoticized and objectified as a thing and not a person. This person's final punch line? "It must be because you're Black!" After they saw the distressed look on my face, I received a beet-faced and embarrassed apology, but by that point, I was stunned into silence. Another person posed the same question to me several days later, following up with the gutting assessment, "I mean you're pretty cute, but not *that* cute."

On a video call my sister asked me jokingly if the rumors about Italian men loving Black women are actually true. I laughed because I knew she was trying to get me to smile and said, "I guess so!" because I wanted to change the subject. There was that insidious word again. "Love." I saw my family for the first time since I left over a month ago in that same video call. They were crowded around the screen, dressed in their Sunday finery, preparing to eat a big dinner after church. My mother was cooking and proudly presented a flat piece of dough to the screen, saying she was making Jamaican fried dumplings in my absence. As they began to sign off, I started to cry. Not just one or two tears but a full-fledged crying jag. Their hearts swelled with what has been the most consistent source of love in my life and they asked me in concerned tones what's wrong. I was in public, at the same bakery that I had repeatedly asked to avoid, and I was bone tired. I wanted to say, "I'm so alone here and I haven't slept well in weeks. I miss you, I miss you, I miss you." But my eyes darted around and connected with the piercing gazes of both the father and the son. They both watched me in my sorrow, my first time crying since I arrived in Italy. I bawled openly and unabashedly, like children do, angry that I could not even have one private moment alone with my sorrow. Instead, I swallowed my sadness and told my family I was just missing them. They told me it would be ok, that I would be home soon. I closed my laptop and resolved not to video chat them again before I went home. I continued to let them hear my voice once a week with phone calls, but they did not see my face again until I disembarked from the plane home. Their eyes were knowing and capable of perceiving the things I wished to hide.

After that, I was silent on the subject of my supposed "admirers" for the remainder of my trip.

* * *

The night before we left the town some sort of festival took over the streets. In a summer filled with more random street fairs and traditional carnivals and open-air markets than I've ever seen before or will likely ever see again, I was relatively indifferent to this latest one. In a city built (literally) on Etruscan ruins and surrounded by preserved medieval walls, it wasn't out of the ordinary to see floats and horse handlers and pigs roasting on a spit in the market for no reason besides the fact that it was a Sunday, and the weather was fair. A sort of rampant racial, ethnic, and nationalist pride seemed to have a firm grip on the imaginations of its inhabitants, many of whom spent their free time dressing up in costumes to preserve their jealously guarded historical narratives. One night, we emerged from the theatre to find men in medieval dress stampeding through the square on horseback. Another night, I listened to an Italian cover band sing a rendition of Jeff Buckley's "Hallelujah" that lasted well over thirty minutes, and another sing an almost incomprehensible rendition of Pink Floyd's "Wish You Were Here." It was a celebration night. The fire for cultural preservation was streaming everywhere in the town. The few teenagers I befriended hated it, longing instead for the international delights of New York and London. However, there was no denying the fervor with which cultural pride seemed to take hold of this place.

So, with this in mind, the festival on the final night seemed set up to be just another in a long line of midsummer diversions. I was not sure exactly what we were celebrating, but it was our last night in town, and we were merry. After four-and-a-half weeks (_____) had gone home. An emergency called her away. As I hugged her fiercely goodbye, my heart ached a bit around the space of her absence. Now, I was truly alone. The remaining crew members had finished packing up for two performances in Pavia, and the bus was leaving early in the morning. As the company sat outside in the same café, I was grateful that I wouldn't be there another day. I would miss the characters in the town, but I was itching for the flow of a city again. I heard that Pavia is a college town, and this made me feel hopeful. A city would mean a place where I could circulate unnoticed again. Or at least less well-noticed.

There was a DJ blasting music in the streets. Because the café was located right below my window, I didn't worry about going home late and unattended. The DJ was blasting the kind of music that I hate. Generic, loud, and mostly American, I refer to this particular genre of music and the type of dancing it inspires as "the grown folks' two-step." Not overtly sexy or risqué, mostly the music requires exaggerated gestures, goofy facial expressions, miming, lip-syncing, and stepping side to side. In short: the type of dancing you would be comfortable doing in front of your entire family at an awkward reunion or a mild-enough wedding.

I can't say my family has ever abided by these rules. I still remember going to the West Indian day parade in New York City with my father and admiring the almost nude bodies of the dancers slowly descending on their haunches to the floor. When I was a kid, my parents loved to dance in the sort of unrestrained way that Caribbean people do, which has everything to do with sex appeal. When I was seven my godmother showed me how to wind my hips in a small circle, my small hands perched on either side of my waist. One night in Italy, my roommate came into our shared bedroom to find me dancing on my bed in the dark. I was listening to hip-hop and dancehall music in my headphones so that she could not hear. It probably looked more like I was writhing around in a fit than dancing.

By the time this last night arrived, I was desperate to dance, even to this. A small group of us took to the floor. We thrust our hips in the twist. We sang loudly and proudly: scolding "Runaround Sue," exclaiming Aretha's "Freedom," and questioning (because we wanna know) "Hey! Baby," will you be my girl? I headed inside to the bathroom and missed one song while waiting in line. It was apparently some sort of line dance, but I didn't know either the song or the steps. I saw my friends get caught up in the whirlwind of movement, jumping high in the air and being swung around by different partners. It was over by the time I returned to the group, and I was thankful.

I have never much cared for line dances. They seem like a place you go to hide amongst the crowd. But isn't half the point of dancing to be seen? How can anyone see your knowing looks and straight legs and curved hips and small smiles if you are all in a line facing forward?

After a few more rounds of this mystery song, the DJ began to play "Cotton Eye Joe." Bolstered by a few glasses of wine and the open air I looked around to see if anyone had started the moves. Most of the faces I saw looked oblivious to both the music and the intended dance and so continued to move in indistinguishable little groups.

I learned about the Cotton Eye Joe dance during an uneventful trip to Girl Scout camp. My mother (the troop leader for several years before she went back to law school) was and remains an unenthusiastic camper. Having grown up in rural Jamaica with a genuine outhouse, no electricity, and no indoor plumbing until her teens, I don't think she ever truly saw the point in paying money for the privilege of having her American children piss outside (as she so aptly put it). One rainy day at camp, we took a square-dancing lesson, and an instructor taught the whole group this stupid dance. Knowing the steps has proven to be a vaguely useful skill at awkward graduation parties and middle school dances. Once, a group of fifteen of us did the Cotton Eye Joe down the aisle at Yankee Stadium to get our faces on the Jumbotron. And it worked. But I can never remember doing this dance with my own family. Amongst ourselves, we mostly consider it a distinctly white American thing. We much prefer the Electric Slide. Did you know the singer is Jamaican?

Standing in Italy on the fresh clay-colored cement tiles recently completed by the male North African day laborers, I felt an unlikely nostalgia for this goofy dance. All at once I began to move.

Heel forward, heel back, outward step, inward step. Heel forward, heel back, outward step, inward step.

As my foot flew up, I slapped my heel the way I learned many years ago. This song is awful. I hate it. But it is familiar and friendly, so I did the steps, making an exaggerated lasso motion over my head each time I turned around in a full circle at the end of the routine. My friends asked me to slow down a moment and teach them. I kicked off my dirty white flip-flops right there in the town square so I could move more freely.

I demonstrated the moves, but not nearly slowly enough, and began to lead the dancing as people from the town stood by staring. Even as I hooted and hollered in the town square, deliberately showing off, I felt the strange onset of longing creeping over me. I had started to form an uncomfortable affinity for this place, despite the pangs of depression I was trying my hardest to disguise.

As my bare feet pounded down on the pavement laid carefully by the men whose eyes I studiously avoided every morning, I whirled in circles beneath a cloud of cigarette smoke and starlight. I know what I must have looked like: barefoot and dirty, the ends of my shirt had come loose from the waistband of my shorts, and I was laughing with my face turned up to the sky. I looked wild and uncaring. It was my last night. A woman pretended to steal my shoes and grabbed my wrists to spin me in a circle. I let her continue the joke a little bit too long, for once unconcerned about the stares I was attracting. As she spun away from me, she kissed me on the cheek, and I was too drunk to care. I twirled deeper into the center of the crowd, still spinning my hands above my head and kicking my bare feet. I closed my eyes and just listened, feeling the weight of the stares from the people standing on the periphery of the square watching the dance floor. I skirted away cautiously from any older men who moved too close, but I smiled at everyone else I saw, from old people enjoying the night air to the teenagers skirting furtively away from their guardians' watchful eyes. In a town this small, there are very few secrets that are well-kept.

Long after everyone else returned to their seats I continued to dance around the square with one of the musicians from our orchestra, a white woman from Scotland. Like me she was young and loved dancing. We were both filled with the energy of the night. I did not attempt to fade away. I danced like I would if I was at home, completely aware of the proud dimensions of my body. I moved my hips the way my godmother taught me, moved my head the way I've seen my mother, and my aunties do. My bare feet felt like they were flying on the cobblestone road, which was curiously still warm from the hot Italian sun, even though this was many hours after sunset. As I spun around, I saw my friend from Palestine, and I joined him. He danced shyly, but we did not care. The three of us were young, from three far-reaching corners of the globe (US, Middle East, and Scotland). We did not say much, just flung our bodies into motion, each of us looking desperately to breathe more air and take up more space. It felt wonderful and perhaps looked like a picture from a catalog, even though it was just for a moment in a forgotten night.

As I rotated in circles, I took stock of the crowd, their faces warping around my whipping head like an overexposed roll of film. I boldly made eye contact with strangers, perhaps for the first time in weeks. I saw the adopted son of the German man

I had met my very first night in town. He watched from the crowd, his dark Black face grinning absently. He smiled at me, at the crowd, at the stupidity of this dance, at the night.

I saw him too.

* * *

We spent a little over a week in scorching hot Pavia, taking the show out for a limited tour. When we arrived, the town looked half-abandoned because approximately 50% of the businesses and homes were shuttered up tight for the summer holidays. More doors than I could count bore signs reading "Closed for the holidays" or "Will return in September." The Italians in our company told us this is fairly common in the Northern cities, which grow particularly hot and unbearable during the late summer months. I wondered where all the people had actually gone, the idea of vacations that stretched over months and weeks instead of days completely baffling me as both an American and the daughter of Caribbean migrants from whom I inherited a secret shame about the sin of idleness. I have always associated long vacations with schoolchildren. As a grad student, my three-month long summer was what allowed me to even join the company for so long. Well, that and my passport. And yet it still baffled me that a town would become almost empty with the only reason being a need to rest.

In town, we stayed in a college dormitory. The buildings were old, musty, and mostly disgusting the way many college dorms are. We suspected that some of the rooms we were assigned were still being occupied by students, with personalized posters on the walls and unfolded linens in the closet. The building was mostly empty of students for the summer, even though Pavia is something of a college town. After I hauled my suitcase slowly up to my seventh-floor room (the elevators were inconveniently out of service) I was surprised to see a half-dressed dark-skinned Black man shaving his head in the sink. He was equally if not more surprised to see me. I wandered down the hall looking for my room and heard languages and voices I did not recognize. Most of the students I encountered who were there for the summer seemed to hail from West Africa. Sometimes they seemed to be speaking Italian or French. Late at night I heard the students laughing together in the communal kitchen on the floor and smelled the strong scent of homemade curries and stews drifting underneath my door. I became accustomed to my tongue cramping with hunger every time I caught a whiff of boiled white rice.

Just like the African migrants in the small town we'd come from, they appeared to view my American accent and inflated unwrapped hair with a hint of curiosity. There were many Black students here from the African continent, causing one member of the company to say, "Look, there are other Black people!" when our bus first pulled into town. I was reminded in that moment of Frantz Fanon's "Look, a negro!"

The students mostly went about their lives as if I didn't exist and I decided to do nothing to impose upon their community. Besides, by this point I was tired. I noticed that they had not gone on three-month long holidays, instead staying behind in dorm rooms without AC that sometimes felt like ovens and were filled to the rafters with vicious mosquitoes. By the end of our stay in town, my body was swollen with bites while their Black skin looked remarkably unaffected. Like my family members in Jamaica, they appeared to have built up resistance to the sticky little bugs and therefore did not swell up like a melon the way I did. My extreme sensitivity to mosquito bites is one of the many "Yankee" things about me that caused mild teasing from my cousins in my childhood. Once I reacted so poorly to the bites that my face was puffy and swollen and a woman on the flight home stopped to ask my mother if I was sick and possibly contagious.

* * *

I do not have much else to say about Pavia. The brevity of our stay there made it impossible to see the whole town. When the rest of the company flew home after the final performance, two other interns and I were still stuck in Italy for a final week. Originally told to book flights for a week after the closing so we could return to strike the set, we were unexpectedly relieved of our duties and told to "explore" for the remainder of our time. Due to insanely restrictive flight alteration policies, I did the math and figured it was actually cheaper to remain in the country for a week than to pay for a new flight home. With this in mind we made a plan to head to Milan, where the prices of hostels in the off-season were low, and the train would allow us to slip over the border into Switzerland for a day before returning us to Rome for our flights home. My company for this final week was two affable white American men from the crew in their early twenties. We had been solid friends for the weeks leading up to this moment, and we settled in our first hostel with glee. It was a tiny studio-style apartment in a beautifully outfitted building with a kitchenette. Finally free from the madness of a production schedule and the confines of our small-town streets, we made up our minds to salvage what was left of our unplanned Italian holiday.

Milan was largely boarded up for the summer months, just like its neighbor, Pavia. On our second morning, two of us set out to see the famous Milanese Duomo, a rather large and impressive Italian cathedral. I stopped by the entrance to take a few panoramic shots. By this point in the trip, I had stepped inside more cathedrals in two months than I had in the entirety of my life. As someone who left her Pentecostal upbringing at age sixteen, it was nevertheless quite a feat for me not to get swept up in the Catholic fervor of the region. Mostly, I was in awe of the structures themselves, their beauty unmarred by the symbolism behind them. I have remained actively spiritual for the entirety of my adult life. But even after abandoning organized religion, my heart has always secretly worshiped the exquisite beauty that often accompanies sacred space. That day, I wasn't so determined to see the outlandish insides of the Duomo, but all the tourist websites we visited advised us to take in Milan's most notable attraction, second only to its extravagant fashion week.

As we approached the entrance, I saw guards standing in wait at the door. At this point, most of my clothes were either dirty or air-drying after being dunked into the sink back at the hostel. The dormitories had no laundry services, and I had just enough clothing and clean underwear to make it to the end of the week. Standing in line with my friend, I wore dark-wash blue jeans cuffed high on my calves to allow greater circulation of air. My arms were bare in a sleeveless shirt that hung loosely off my body before ending in a deliberately uneven hem past my hips. I saw many white European women with rosary beads in long skirts, ranging in age from infancy to ancient. These comprised the lines of the faithful.

Amongst their numbers were tourists like us, here only to gawk at the high ceilings and priceless art. I saw more than one woman cease her praying to extract a long, silken scarf or a small shrug from the interior of her purse. These were thrown up high in the air and allowed to drift slowly back down to their heads or wrapped firmly around their waists to conceal what little expanses of skin were visible to the naked eye. When we reached the gate the guard stopped us with the flat palm of his hand, pointing to a white sign depicting men and women with big red *X*'s and stop signs emblazoned over their faces. According to the images, clothes that are considered too revealing are grounds for being barred from entry. The guard pointed again to my bare shoulders and instructed me to get out of the line. I looked around and saw approximately 50% of the women being turned away, ones who (like me) were unaware of the dress code. My friend was wearing shorts and a t-shirt. Without missing a step, he went inside without me, tossing back over his shoulder for me to wait outside.

When my friend returned, I was tired. The sun was getting lower, so we made up our minds to walk home.

On our first three days in Milan, we ate in a restaurant offering a three-course meal for ten euros. Eating at this point more for economy than pleasure, we returned for the abundance of the food (which filled us up all day) and the friendliness of the staff, who offered us the password to the wireless internet they had hooked up in the apartment the owner lived in upstairs. They also gave us their lovely smiles. It was at this moment that I realized how much our movements had centered on finding free internet, the one faithful connection we each had to home. It made negotiating the terrain that much harder since we have all grown rather stupid in the age of smartphones. We got lost more often than not, stopping strangers to timidly ask for directions by repeating the names of our intended locations over and over again. We learned "left" and "right." We learned when to shut up. I became an expert at reading subtle looks of exasperation on strangers' faces who clearly thought we must be very stupid to disembark without directions.

On the occasion of our third and final meal in our new favorite restaurant, we were laughing with our waiter about New York. He knew more English than we knew Italian and asked things about the New York Yankees and skyscrapers. He was a middle-aged and friendly Italian man with deep, dark tan skin like he had spent many hours in the sun. I thought this was rather strange for someone who worked primarily indoors. The meal came with coffee, and so after catching my breath from laughter, I held up three fingers to indicate that we would each like one. He bowed with a dish towel over the crook of his arm in an overly demonstrative gesture of deference. I laughed again, delighting in his quick humor and movements.

He ran inside and returned with three beautifully arranged cups, filled to the brim with smoking hot steamed milk and coffee. He had taken care with each cup, perching a little spoon on the edge of each saucer, the weight of the spoons holding down our individual sugar packets, even though there was plenty of sugar on the table already. I knew he had done all of this because he liked us and wanted to see us smiling again. Because we came here every day and ordered the same thing but still tipped him very well, the way American tourists want to do.

The cups were gleaming white. Staring back at me were six identical jet-black faces, one on each cup and one on each sugar packet. Their lips were fiery red like cherries but designed to mirror the shape of coffee beans. Their bugging white, white eyes were looking off to the side, as if they were too stupid to comprehend something very simple. The tops of their heads were crowned with tight kinky coils so dark in shade they matched the unnatural tarring of their faces. Blackface.

Here I was again, without words.

I looked back at our waiter. At home I would have caused a scene. At home I would have walked out. At home I would have known why he gave us these cups, what he intended to say to me that he did not need to say to my white male companions in their early twenties. At home I might have raised my voice, or dropped it down real low with the seething tone of disgust I learned from my mother when I was young. I would have humiliated him for hurting me.

I looked up from the surface of my cup, my eyes blurring against the heat of the milk until I could barely see the light dusting of cocoa floating across the thin skin forming on the surface. The cocoa he put there because he liked me and wanted, somehow, for me to be happy. He was distressed to see me tearing up, and his face crumpled into a look of truly genuine concern. I realized then that he did not understand my offense, even though part of me can never truly like him again. He leaned down near me to ask if we needed something else, and I thought, "This man is not that good of an actor. I don't think he knows." I could not give rise to my indignation, so I consumed it whole. I thanked him for the cups and turned away. I did not speak to him again when he returned to the table with the bill; I did not look in his eyes. I turned my chin high in indignation and do not remember if I left a tip, even though I know it is unlikely that he even purchased these stupid mugs or even chose to use them that day. I looked around and saw them dotting the surfaces of almost every other table in the outdoor seating area. He made a few more quick jokes, but I could no longer laugh. I saw his confusion at my rejection, but I would not concede.

At a loss for what to do I turned to my friends. Their shifting backsides and darting glances were almost too much for me to bear. They both made light of our fine china and delicately sipped their coffee, afraid to look too eager. I could not touch the cup.

I took out my phone and snapped a picture of mine in the way it was presented to me. I posted it online. In the caption I wrote:

"What exactly do you say when you get coffee served in a cup like this?"

I waited patiently as my phone began to ring, signaling the incoming flood of responses. This was the first truly negative or distressed thing I had posted online since my arrival here nearly two months ago. Before now every picture was:

Me and (_____) arm in arm at the cathedrals of Orvieto and Perugia.

Me perched high up on the walls over Assisi.

Me smiling back over my shoulder in the pressing streets of Florence.

Me leaning against the rails of various docks, pathways, and historic streets.

Me in our small town drinking amber beer surrounded by strangers and friends (most of whom I knew I would never see again).

There was no room in the caption to provide all of my own answers, so I simply asked the question. It was not a rhetorical question, so I waited and did not touch the cup.

Responses ranged from the hysterical, to the uncomfortably unfunny, to deep internet outrage. One friend posted a link to an article about racist caricatures in cities around the world and I thanked him. Another insisted that I refuse to pay for it and a handful of people agreed by liking her post. I knew this would not happen. I would not walk out of there without payment, knowing I was more likely to end up in a confrontation with the managers and the Italian police than I was to be offered an apology. Part of me had to simply ignore this option. I knew I would pay for the cup.

After the better part of an hour the milk in my cup had congealed and gone stone cold. I sat smoking and waited, for what I was unsure. I only knew that if I did not get it, I would ash my cigarettes in the now pitiful cappuccino, settle the bill, and be on my way. The staff did not mind that we lingered so long. After all, we were regulars.

My phone rang one more time. I received this response written by my beloved college advisor:

Wow. Actually, I think you have to say a lot, a whole lot. How about an essay about what it has been like to travel and work in Italy as a Jamaican American woman, both the good and the bad (and the ugly). What has it been like being there during Minister Kyenge's ordeals? Have you met any black immigrants & if not what does that say about Italians and about study/work abroad from US institutions? I think there is still a need for institutions to think more about how travel in Europe and South America is experienced differently by folks of color because of the way race functions abroad. I am glad so many of your days in Italy have been inspiring and I hope this is a cup of coffee you can mull over and brew into something fierce.

Sorry about the typos!

This was what I had been waiting for, although I did not know it then. She told me what I needed to hear, gave me my medicine like an expert physician. She told me to write.

It was several hours before I could force the lump in my throat down far enough to send her my grateful reply. I knew what I had to do. Ashing the last of my menthol cigarettes into our communal ashtray I picked up the cup. I drank the now unappealing contents down in one long, strong gulp, and felt it settle in the base of my stomach. I wiped my lips, and we went home to our studio with the tidy tiny kitchenette. I offered to cook meals for our remaining days here in Milan in order to save money from the restaurant, and the men I was with readily agreed, offering in turn to wash the plates.

* * *

236

We were finally heading home.

After a week in Milan, one of our little trio had finally departed, able to change his flight to leave from the airport here instead of from Rome. My final companion and I were not so lucky. After the first few nights, we checked out of our well-appointed hotel and moved about a mile across town to an older, historic hotel. Looking at the hordes of idlers on the streets I saw that we were now more centrally located in the heart of Milan. The hotel was musty with an aging air conditioning unit that made the surface of my skin feel clammy rather than cool. The room was so tight that only the overly large double bed and one nightstand could comfortably fit inside. This was the only hotel I have ever stayed in that asked us to return the keys to the front desk every time we left. The doors were so old it required a special combination of tricks to jimmy the lock, even with the correct key. The keys themselves looked normal but were attached to a heavy keychain that weighed approximately one pound, supposedly a deterrent to stop key theft.

For the second time in two months, I caved and bought McDonald's. When my companion shamed me about eating American fast food, I raised my eyebrows at him and pointed out that the restaurant was full of Italians and other foreign nationals and that we were two of the only Americans inside. At this, he blushed slightly, and I ordered my Big Mac without shame. In line behind me, I saw three dark Black faces, two men and one woman. The woman's hair was pulled back in cornrows that fell in cascading lengths of hair extensions down her back. The men had close-cropped fades and were wearing very large basketball jerseys with American team names emblazoned on the front. I heard them giggling behind me, making gestures in a huge halo around their faces to indicate my hair. One (I think the woman) extended a hand close to my nape. I sensed it more than saw it and shifted from one foot to the next, hearing the grasping arm fall back against the thigh of the unseen offender with a faint slapping sound. In all my months here, I was ashamed that I could not distinguish various African languages, and so I cannot truly tell you where they were from. Until now, I usually depend on the colonial language of the Black bodies around me (English, Spanish, Italian, French) to help determine rough geographical placements. Here in Milan, this was no longer applicable, the multiple languages on the street making my head swim and ache until I stopped focusing so intently, realizing my efforts were useless. I could not and need not capture everything I see, despite my best efforts.

I knew this group was not curious about my hair's texture, which mirrored perfectly their own. It was more the style and the length that seemed to catch their eye. I do not know. I accepted my food at the counter and smiled timidly at the floor as I left. The woman smiled broadly, and the men remained straight-faced as they watched me go.

In the subway, they were broadcasting news of Minister Kyenge on a series of TV screens. I saw a blonde, tattooed white woman with strings of facial piercings watching it intensely and periodically glaring over her shoulder at me. The heated hatred in her eyes startled me, but I did not flinch or turn my eyes. Clutching my McDonald's bag, I scanned the crowd quickly and saw I was not the only Black woman on this platform. But I was just the one she noticed first. Again, I wondered if my appearance screamed "American" to her. We hastily ducked inside the car of the train when it arrived.

Earlier in the week, before the third member of our trio had departed, a swaying Black woman with far-off distant eyes that spoke of either addiction or instability asked us loudly on the train if we believed in JESUS CHRIST. I said no and returned my eyes to my hands while she continued at length in a variety of tongues (some real and others brought on by the holy ghost) about the pride and sin of the non-believer, pointing downwards at my seat. She asked my friend if he believed in CHRIST, and he said yes. I do not know if this is true or if he simply wanted her to go away since he was raised Jewish. My second friend agreed with the first. Apparently, they were now both avid followers of JESUS CHRIST, OUR LORD AND SAVIOR. However, I would not relent, not even to make her happy and not even to send her away. She turned to ask me again, and I repeated my steady no, lifting my chin to look at the opposite wall of the car. I shouldn't have been so cool with her as she was not in her right mind, but I could not let another person shame me on this trip. Plus my relationship to the Divine was mine and mine alone to question. I learned years ago to stop letting others' shame dictate my relationship with my creator.

In the train station in Milan, we encountered the usual mundane traveler's anxiety ("Who printed the tickets? Did you print the tickets? Where are the tickets?!") Rushing over to the kiosk we were immediately surrounded by a small flock of dark-skinned Black men. I had seen them all week, hanging back beside the ticketing stations, offering their help with the counterintuitive machines in exchange for tips. I wondered how much money they made with this system of exchanging "favors" as their primary mode of labor. They switched rapidly between multiple languages, and I caught small phrases of English, Italian, French, Spanish, and what sounded to me like German, as well as conversing privately with each other in words and languages I did not know. Although I refused their offer, I stood back to watch them hustle, moving briskly from potential customer to potential customer. I was stunned by the quick fluency of their tongues and compared this moment to my own experience in the Roman airport a full two months ago: my tentative Italian, the confident but sometimes limited English of the designated tourist guides. I saw these men weaving intricately back and forth, changing directions as often as they changed tongues and I change moods, their brightly colored polos and loose denim jeans sporting brand names. They moved with confident ease from tourist to tourist, only displaying their anxieties openly amongst themselves.

We boarded the train with little incident. Our seats faced each other, with a window and another set of seats on our left and two small airline-style tables in between us. On my right sat a lanky, blonde, teenage white girl in a small-cropped t-shirt and stonewashed denim shorts faded under deliberate factory-manufactured distress. She was sitting next to a man who looked like her father, flipping disinterestedly through her phone. I thought, "She doesn't look Italian. Maybe American or British?" to myself as I slid into the seat that faced her across the aisle. I don't know why it became so important to me to place and name people throughout that trip, but I couldn't seem to stop the habit.

Minutes before we were destined to launch, an elderly Black woman boarded the train pulling the hand of a small, reluctant dark-skinned girl child. I could not tell if she was pouting or if that expression was caused by the swollen fat cheeks of her pretty toddler face forcing her lips into a pucker. She had a denim blue bucket hat pulled over her eyes and could not see very clearly where her caretaker was leading her. The old woman decided that it would be easier to pull their luggage if she didn't also have to drag the child and so she nudged her forward with the flat palm of her hand, directing her to climb into the appropriate set of seats before the white man sitting across from her stood up to help her with their bags. I was warmed to see that someone did what I was already getting ready to do myself.

The woman's floor-length skirt, bandana-covered head, and plain blue t-shirt top reminded me of my older female relatives in Jamaica who always pinch my fat and tell me I'm a nice girl. My parents' older cousins. My great-grandma. My father's aunt who lived in the rural country and had no teeth as long as he knew her but loved to kiss my face with soft wet lips and gums because she only wore her dentures for church. They all have names that sound sweet and light on the lips. Ivy. Ines. Bev. Dassa. Putus (pronounced puh-toos, the accent falling on the second syllable) is the one who had no teeth.

On the train this brisk granny ushered the child into her seat, forcing her to sit still and remove her hat. The child's head was patchy but completely bald as if it was regularly shaved but hadn't been in a while. In certain spots her caretaker had placed small accenting plastic jewels that the girl fiddled with between her chubby fingers. I have always saved the softest corner of my heart for small children. The softest corner of that soft corner is reserved for Black girls, especially when their faces are fat, and their eyes are so wonderfully bright.

This little Black girl could not be contained for long. She flipped her hat into the vacant seat next to her and frequently slipped into the traffic of the aisle when her grandmother was not looking. Although I could see the grandmother clearly, the little girl's back was facing me so that half of the time I could not read her expressions.

While the man was lifting their luggage into the overhead rack, she seized her opportunity to explore. With the tip of her pudgy thumb pursed in her lips she saw me first. She stopped, blinking but mostly unimpressed by the picture I presented her with. I smirked at her boldness and offered her a little wink, which made her sulky lips smile around her short thumb. In each of her earlobes, she wore two glistening gold earrings that winked back at me in the sunlight through the window, making her face shine above the flaming red color of her shirt and her white-sandaled feet.

Turning from me she looked at the head of the blonde-haired teenager on my right with bored eyes and a mobile phone. I say she looked at her head because the clinical light in her eyes seemed to focus only on the hair. She did not attempt to round the corner and see the girl's face. She did not attempt to meet her eyes. She simply crept forward, shyly, to examine the qualities of her two-plus feet of pin-straight blonde hair. She looked at it once with the shrewd assessment of an old-fashioned barber and wig maker. Reaching out with her free hand she flicked the tail end of it once to the left and then back again to the right, as if she was running her hands through hanging threads of beads. Casually she ran her knuckles through its length, letting the strands of blonde slip between the fingers of her outstretched hand. All the while she never removed her eyes from me, measuring my response with eerily piercing intelligence. I offered her no explanations outside of my growing smile.

The teenager noticed the tugging almost immediately, glancing down over her shoulder to look at the girl. Following the direction of her gaze she then looked at me too. I did not know what to say so I smiled at her, and she returned the gesture. She must have thought the little girl was mine. We both watched, rapt, as the little Black girl continued to run her short fingers in and out of the white teenager's hair, testing its mass on the flat palm of her upturned hand.

We began to move, the train creeping forward in a slow start. Back from dealing with the safe storage of their bags, the granny made a soft hissing sound by sharply drawing the air in between her bared teeth. She gently took the girl by the upper arm and returned her to her seat, fussing over her t-shirt, extracting her thumb, and running work-weathered palms over the surface of her mostly smooth head.

I extracted a well-worn copy of Toni Morrison's *Sula* from my bag in preparation for the journey. Once we had settled, the train gathered speed, and the little Black girl twisted around in her seat one final time to touch the heavy falls of the white girl's blonde hair. Again, the teenager looked at me with a self-conscious smile and I gave the little girl a none-too-harsh look of disapproval I reserved for my baby cousins, indicating with a small twirling motion of my index finger that she should face forward in her seat. Her granny saw and smiled. In a grand finale of defiance, the girl used her own index finger to give the blonde hair one final mighty flick, returning her thumb to her puckered mouth before facing straight ahead.

Looking to my left I watched as the train emerged on the surface streets of Milan, speeding forward towards Rome and the plane that would take me eventually home. Closing my eyes and my book, I returned it to the confines of my purse, choosing instead to cross my arms over the dry, hard surface of the little train tray table, creating an awkward human pillow and blanket. I bowed my head into the hollows of my arms, allowing my nose to inhale deeply from the warm crooks of my elbows, drifting into a sleep that is never fully settled or easy, and sighed.

I had finally grown accustomed to the weightiness of things.

* * *

My whole life I have been made to feel like a thing in a jar. The jar itself is glass, brittle, and translucent, mirroring the fragility of its contents.

In the end and in part this is a story about pressing my skin flush against the sides of that glass jar and feeling the faint heat of many hands radiating back at me. I also hear the syncopated tap-tap-tapping of probing fingers troubling its smooth surface. I have recorded a few of them here.

I do not know the truth of it. I do not want to know the truth of it. I will never claim that. I simply want to measure the distance between my flesh and the glass, the glass and those hands, those hands and my skin.

Eulogy for a Friend

Dear Friend,

Dear friend.

Dear, dear friend.

Beloved friend.

I just received news of your dying in a dream. When I woke up with a start, I was surprised to discover tears on my cheeks in the fresh light of morning. Who dreams of a loved one's demise? I am glad morning also found you alive and likely in your bed. When you told me recently that you were desperate, wrapped in sadness, and that you wanted to kill yourself, I thought, "How selfish of them to leave me behind." I am always afraid of being left out, or left to wander, or left behind. I selfishly want to live. I want you to live for me, alongside me, with me, around me, even in spite of your suffering.

I have written your name on paper and burned it before. Made of your name an offering to the Deity so that he might still your hand and spare your life. I imagine the Deity laying hands on your body, lifting up the knife, pills, gun, and toxins that you intended to use to end your life force. I plead with the universe to:

Uncock the gun.

Take away the knife.

Unswallow the pills.

Exhale the toxins.

Lift up a life from the ashes of the dead.

I had schooled my heart in ways to miss you long before you contemplated knife ends and suicide. I have trained myself to mourn you even though you are still here. I remembered a boy I barely knew from my childhood who put a gun to his chest and blew away his insides. In the aftermath of a gunshot, I thought, "His poor parents," prioritizing their grief over his passing. Maybe that is what I am most afraid of. That if you end your own life people will forget that you were full of mischief and laughter, quick to say I love yous, grumpy and small at times, and deliriously alive. People will tut their tongues and say, "Their poor parents/friends/lovers/acquaintances." They will misplace their pity because they will know that you did this to yourself. I live in fear of a late-night phone call from some anonymous voice telling me that you are gone, that you have succeeded where I wished so desperately for you to fail. I think of all these things, and feel all of these things, and say all of these things now in preparation for the end, even though you are not dead yet.

Your suicidality, friend, took me by surprise when you first told me. It felt like my heart string was attached on one end to my chest and on the other end to a sadly deflating balloon, sinking slowly back to earth. The slack heartstring is no longer taut enough to carry the balloon onward. I am wondering if I should cut it and see how far it can float.

I have always been in love with the life of you. The air of purpose surrounding you, even in the sad silence. I have experienced loss without you, and I will experience it again when you are gone. But I am living in the wake of this dream death, and its attendant sadness. I am living so that I can bury my dead.

Lift up the body.

Lay down the burden.

Raise up a life from the ashes of the dead.

I imagine a false memory of us laughing, or camping, or biking, or shopping, or singing, or sitting deliberately still. I imagine us rapt as we listen to each other and make up our minds that we want to live, if for nothing else but the love of one another. As if love is a stable and steady thing. As if love can keep us alive. I summon you now in your sadness to say that there is a life beyond despair. There is a way to come home to yourself.

In Greek mythology, Antigone is forbidden from burying her brother, on pain of immediate death. And still she buries him, gathering up fistfuls of dirt to enshrine his body in soil and earth.

In my dream last night, I was at your funeral, shocked at the thinness of the crowd and that they could give the final religious rites to suicidal sinners. I always assumed when I was young and suicidal that my body would become a discarded thing, naked of Earth and left to rot in the winds like Antigone's brother. Perhaps there is no rhyme or reason to my fears, except for the fact that sometimes evil prevents us from burying our dead. There is nothing unnatural about death and yet it often feels unjust.

Raise up the body.

Settle the bones.

Make mourning an action of both spirit and flesh.

Sometimes it feels to me as if certain people are stalked by death. This makes me short tempered and angry. Why can't death wait its turn? Instead, it casts a dim shadow over them that never goes away. In my life I have had a surplus of love, an embarrassment of affection. And even so, I am worried that when I die there will be no one left to tend to my body if I take my life. No one left to remember that I was quick to say I love you, ambitious and anxious, (hopefully) kind.

Who will keep watch over our bodies when we are gone? Who will remember us, my friend? Who will tend to the bodies that housed us and carried us through this world? It is telling of the living what they do with their dead. When you died in my dreams last night you returned as a phantom. No one had tended to your remains. No one had scooped up a fistful of dirt to sprinkle over your body, to signal to the Deity that you had been laid to rest. I want you to rest.

And so I say:

When you die ...

Before I die ...

Before we both die ...

If I survive you ...

I will bury you, I will bury you, I will bury you.

What good will my mental health do me at the end of the world?

I don't mean to take on and carry on as if I'm dying (Death after all is an immutable fact of living, for the ability to die is the surest sign of life.) But what good will my mental health do me at the end of the world?

The world, in its finite spherical shape, lacks the definitive ends of its more linear and angular cousins. And yet it will end and all I will be left with are the deep breathing exercises a therapist taught me in grad school to manage my anxious insides. But shouldn't I be nervous?

The world, after all, is ending.

The end of the world may feel much less catastrophic than I originally thought it would. People are in the streets (But they were always in the streets.) The masses are starving and sad from the hunger they've nursed for a lifetime. We play the stories on the news as if we have to have a living record for generations who will not come. And even if they do, they will not be given the grace of old age.

I do not fancy myself unique in my concerns. In fact my doom is ever-present and commonplace. I hope the end of the world is sudden, unexpected, and painless (Which is almost a guarantee that it will be prolonged, painful, and predicted.) I've heard if you brace your body for impact you risk wounding yourself even more during the fall.

Send me plagues and politics, wars and witchcraft. You know, the things that kill off populations in one fell swoop. At the end of the world I'll be meditating and trying to manage my heartbeat as the tanks of tyranny roll down the streets below my window. I'll be listening to lo-fi hip-hop focus music and clearing out my email inbox. Or dreaming of the perfect dirty chai latte from the coffee shop where I used to go and write things down but now there is only so much rubble.

Where can I do yoga during the apocalypse? Where can I buy scented candles? Will I remember to only use "I" statements as they are killing us?

"I believe that …"

"I feel that …"

"I wish you wouldn't …"

Ok that last one is a bad example since it gives "you" a directive.

I don't imagine there will be podcasts or long baths or brisk walks outdoors after the revolution. I don't imagine there will be much at all. This includes me.

But I hope that …

I hope that …

I hope that there may be some semblance of music for me to dance to or cry to or at least to punctuate the hours as I sit on the lawn and stare directly into an unforgiving sun drawing us closer and closer to its fatal orbit.

I hope I am wearing soft clothes and comfortable shoes. Or perhaps more realistically I will be naked and shamelessly whispering mantras, "I am enough, I am worthy, I have always been enough," even up until the last conscious moment of this world yields back into the nothingness of the universe.

I hope I remember my breathing exercises then.

An Essay for My Body as Triptych

"Everybody here is infirm."

—*Gwendolyn Brooks*

PART I: BONE BLACK INFIRMITIES

I am taking a taxi to a train to somewhere new when I see the man. I am riding in the back of the taxi and trying my hardest to make small talk. To be honest the talk with my taxi driver is *painfully small*. These are the conversations I hate the most. "What do you do?" "Where are you headed?" "You from around here?" These things are not nearly noteworthy enough to sustain a conversation and yet I feel compelled to politely oblige when I am in close proximity to a talker. I do not want them to think I am rude, even though these social graces do not come easily to me. I turn my head to the side to fiddle in my bag for my wallet when we arrive at the station, and I see a dark-skinned Black man scouring the sidewalk near the bus stop. It is clear to me that he is not well. His black clothing is so dirty that you can see the spots against the dark background, even though it is commonplace knowledge that black clothing hides dirt. I assume he is looking for a cigarette, a sight that is familiar to me after four years of living in the economically disparate world of New Haven, with the overwhelming privilege of Yale on the one hand and the struggles of the community on the other. I assume he is looking for a cigarette butt that is not too burned down, because I have seen many people do this exact same thing before. He will smoke the ash end and then look for another one. Or perhaps he is searching for change, although this seems the less likely of the two options since there's rarely any change to be found but plenty of cigarette butts.

I pay for the cab, and when I return my wallet to my bag, I see the man outside of the window again. He has given up his search, and now he is masturbating, his hand moving furiously inside the loose confines of his overly large and filthy sweatpants. Two other Black men stand by, dressed in the reflective vests and hardhats of construction workers, and laugh at him as he passes. His hand beats a furious rhythm against the front surface of his thigh, and his eyes are far away as if he is dissociated from his own pleasure or as if pleasure isn't even a part of the equation. He does not stop walking to finish his task, instead moving past the bus stop and the front doors of the station and down the sidewalk until I cannot see him anymore. My immediate reaction lies somewhere between revulsion and pity. I am angry that this man is doing this thing, this thing we consider dirtier than his clothes, in public. I am nervous and I wait until he is further down the sidewalk before

I exit the car on the opposite side and hurry into the station. And I am sad. His eyes are glazed and glassy.

He is not well.

What is the solution for this man? To call his family? Does he have a family? Someone to love him or to restrain him or to force him to keep up a strict regimen of medication? Why is it that I assume he does not have these things? If he does have access to these things, does he even want them? Would he refuse if presented with paths to wellness?

He is unwell.

What could someone like me do? Call the police on him? Sentence him to time in the solitary darkness of a jail cell? Create a statistic? Withhold understanding? Withhold care? Is that what he is entitled to? Is that even a solution?

I have been unwell.

I think surreptitiously about the medication in my luggage. The ones designed to control my moods and alter the effects of depression and psychosis. I think of the ones who love me and the clinicians who care. They are the ones who convinced me not to be ashamed that I needed the pills. I found out five years later, when I was twenty-nine, that I would need these pills forever and that I would never be cured. What the clinicians thought was the anxiety and depression of grad school turned out to be bipolar depression 1, incurable and chronic.

There is no difference between this man and me except for access to intervention. But then again, I am assuming he does not have access. I can never really know. I never attempted to know. I snuck out on the far side of the cab to avoid knowing. Maybe I am part of the problem. I avert my eyes from the sight I do not want to see and should not be forced to see. It burns against the surfaces of my mind. It is not that I do not want to see unbridled illness. Or maybe that is precisely the point? I feel ill-equipped to negotiate the terrains of others' diseases. I can barely manage my own.

I have spent my life in conflict with my body. Conflict with my mood disorder but also with this fat, Black, woman, queer, immigrant's daughter, American body that I am blessed with. I have spent years at war trying to feel something different or better or sustainable in any way possible. That man at the station scared me to my core. Was this my future? Old-time church people in my childhood would often say, "There but for the grace of God go I." Is that where I am destined to go without pills and health care and money to pay for pills and health care?

When I was between thirteen and sixteen years old I spent summers in the Bronx working as a volunteer, first in the Ear, Nose, and Throat Department and later in the psychiatric ward's pharmacy. A lifelong nail-biter, I stopped the summer I worked in the psych ward because I was scared I would ingest the dust from the antipsychotics and anti-depressant pills I spent hours sorting and discarding. On one of my first days at work in my first summer as a volunteer, I received a call from a woman requesting more painkillers after surgery. I told her the script that I had studiously memorized from orientation: I was not a medical professional and could not dispense medication or medical advice, but I would see if one of the doctors would speak to her. Please hold.

After punching the button on the keyboard to mute my end of the conversation and lull her with Muzak, I turned to one of the doctors standing over my shoulder, explained to her the situation, and asked if she would like to speak to the patient. She responded by telling me to take a message, that the woman was "probably just a junkie" since it was a "bad sign" when they go through medication "so quickly like that" (To this day I do not know how she would know how quickly or not the woman had taken her medication). I was advised to tell the woman to eat some popsicles. I took a message for the call. Years later I am a grad student at Yale and about two months out from major surgery. Without even thinking my physician writes me a prescription for oxycodone, enough to get me through the recovery, and perhaps even a little more than I need. She explains that it is because it would probably be easier for me to fill it out in the pharmacy downstairs that day than to wait until the day of surgery. I am surprised. I guess a Yale grad student can't be considered "probably just a junkie." (This is all before the backlash and the widespread publicizing of the opioid crisis.)

Days later I returned to New Haven on the train. I saw the man again. It was as if he had been standing there since I left him. He was smoking a fruity-smelling cigarillo and wearing different clothes, this time gray to match the sky. He did not look as dirty as he had before. His eyes were still far away but somehow more focused and his head bore a small white bandage on the left temple. This small sign of caring, that someone had seen him suffering and thought to dress his injury, relaxed me. And yet there was something unsavory about my interest in him. "There but for the grace of God go I."

I want to remove the dressing and examine the wound.

PART II: INSIDE

The bright light of a department store. We are a mother and her two daughters. We are here today to buy a dress for the mother's dead sister. The dress must be respectful and white. It must also be a little bit larger than the size of her body so that the workers at the funeral home in Jamaica can manipulate the sister's limbs, now stiff with death, into the sleeves and long skirt. It must also look like something she would wear in life, although she no longer has any say. The two daughters are teenagers, sisters themselves, and there to accompany their mother. There is a weight, heavy as a stone made smooth by the flowing river, that hangs like an albatross around their collective necks, ringing us lifeless in the store. We do not speak.

The teenage sisters always fight good-naturedly about which one of them looks more like their mama. At this moment, the sisters do not bicker. We all barely breathe. Standing in the white light of the department store, the mother's eye catches her reflection in the mirror. In it, she is holding up a white dress at arm's length. Caught in the reflection, we all freeze, conscious for the first time of the task at hand. There is a schism occurring in the mother, here to buy the respectable white dress they will shroud her dead sister in before laying her to rest, beloved. The daughters recognize this schism and silently call on the resilience of the collective "we." When they speak, it is as if to say, "We have come to buy the dress. We are here together." We are here, in benediction and love, all of us reflected back in the infinite unfolding of department store mirrors.

The younger daughter (the one who lives inside the "I") read once that they turn up the lights in department stores so that you can see yourself more clearly in the mirrors and feel inspired to buy the things you do not need. The light does not inspire us to impulse shop this day, because on this day what we need is each other.

The mother looks at herself again holding the dress of death and begins to cry. The older daughter quietly tells her to give us the money and to go wait in the car. We two daughters will buy the dress. It is the first time the younger daughter can remember seeing her mother cry. Cancer took her sister young. It seems that something is always taking one of us young.

As the mother returns to the car, the sisters wait silently in line. We buy the dress, tell the cashier to just put it in the bag, that we don't need a hanger. Watch her place it carefully in the bag, all folded up as if it is for a special occasion. We return to the car and to our mother with our purchase. The younger daughter takes a moment to understand loss. It is somewhere between the white light and the infinite reflection of the mirrors. She writes a poem for the funeral (Which she is sure they do not read.) Because she is young and in school, and the funeral is far away where her mother grew up, she cannot attend. The younger daughter who lives inside the "I" does not cry, even though she misses her aunt.

* * *

Before any of the children in our family were born, our father lost first his father and then his younger sister to brain aneurysms. They passed suddenly one after the other with no warning. When I am twenty-four and admitted to the psychiatric hospital, they slide my head inside an MRI machine and take a picture of my brain. They take pictures from different angles and vantage points, and show me the images of the spongy surfaces of my mind. They cannot find any evidence of aneurysms inherited from my kinfolk, or any physiological reason for my psychotic break. Part of me is scared that they will tell me I am dying on the inside. The other part of me is anxious to see if I am.

It is not the first time they have turned the camera on my interior. X-rays of my legs and teeth. MRIs of my womb, my whole body submerged in the coffin-like machine. They pipe in music while I'm trapped in there and tell me not to breathe too hard, so I won't mess up the image. Ultrasound wands rubbed over my belly and stuck up inside the empty space of my vagina. Photographs of my inflamed ovaries. I have seen my insides and edges from every angle. I wonder often about the difference a camera would have made for my paternal grandfather and my aunt. What if they could have seen their tender spongy insides? The transparency of bones and fragile teeth? The moon-like surface of the mind? Would it have saved their lives? So many people in my family died young and wanted nothing more than to desperately live and here I am, their sad descendant so hell-bent on premature death. I look at the craters of my brain and wonder if I am heading the same way as them. If the organ I admire most, the thing that gives me my humor and sharp tongue, will one day give out and betray me.

* * *

Earlier the same year of the brain scan I am sitting in the
OBGYN's office and crying because the doctor tells me I will
have to be put under anesthesia for major surgery. My fear of
being put under dates back to my summers spent as a volunteer
worker in a hospital in the Bronx. A woman in the operating
room began to go into cardiac arrest and there was a flurry
of action as physicians and nurses rushed to her aid. I stood,
useless in my ineptitude, watching as they went to struggle
for her life. She died on the operating room table, an allergic
reaction to anesthesia claiming her life. I relived this moment
over and over again in the subsequent months, and it springs
to mind every time I am faced with a needle. I imagine what
this woman looked like, although I have never seen her face. In
my mind's eye she shares my brown complexion and afro curls,
spread out with a halo of light around her now lifeless face. She
looks more like a character in a play than a real person with
dreams and dimensions. I cannot imagine her complexity.

In the doctor's office, I suck in short, shallow breaths and
imagine the tears flowing backwards into the tender insides
of my eyes, my body absorbing and redistributing the sorrow,
breaking it down like roughage. Gnawing on this feeling, I
know that even if I manage to cut and swallow it, it will just
pass undigested through my body like corn. This disgusting
image makes me smile secretly to myself through the fear.
Nervously I flex my right-hand fingers around the edges of the
table while my left hand is engaged in a furious game of catch
and release with the hem of my skirt. Carefully I gather the
edges of the fabric into little pleats, working hard to make each
neat new pleat the same size as the last. I learned this skill from
the (few) times I ironed my school skirt as a girl. Yet this model
is much smaller, each pleat only about as wide as the half-moon

of my longest fingernail and measuring less than a centimeter in length. But it gives me something to do.

The kind-faced white woman obstetrician who has been assigned to remove the cyst from my right ovary is losing me to the whirring chaos of my escalating thoughts. I sense an almost imperceptible shift in her mannerisms meant to reflect patience and reassurance. I do not want the reassuring hand she lays familiarly on my quivering shoulder, careful to apply little to no pressure. I want her to be competent. I want her not to kill me while I'm sedated, or to slip up and leave me spayed like a randy bitch that uselessly humps all the good pillows in the house when company comes, confused and agitated. After all, the cyst on my ovary is large but benign. I sign the release form with hands made stiff from tension, carefully reading the terms as if I'm signing my life away into her hands, which I am.

"They can be rather ... interesting."

The physician speaks these words to my flexing hand and pleating fingers before looking back at me. I am confused at first, wondering what she could possibly be talking about now that the endless stream of release forms for major surgery has finally concluded.

"The cysts. They can grow to be rather, you know, interesting."

And now she has me and she knows it. Her face lifts into a half-smile and she reaches under her medical supply cart with its vast array of instruments designed to barely fit inside of a human vagina and brings out a large hardcover book. It looks like something that would grace the tables of people without very many social skills, so it seems unsurprising to me that my physician would produce it now. Opening it up to the pre-marked section on dermoid cysts (Was it her who carefully dog-eared the appropriate page?), she holds the book flat on its spine for my inspection. Now the thing inside of me that my parents labeled "inquisitive" when I was a child and others "rude" and "prying" in my adulthood begins to peek its shy head up to the surface. I have always been naturally curious about anatomy and biology. In fact, it was this fascination that led me to believe that I would be a doctor from age four until nineteen. Then one day in sophomore year of college I walked up to my biology instructor in the lab, told her I was never coming back, and stayed true to my word. Pursuing a major in the arts, that I secretly feared at first was a waste of what other people labeled my "potential," I approached books and art and literature with the same surgical precision of my anatomy dissections. I wanted to split them open on their spine and investigate their insides. To understand them.

So here is the inquisitive little girl, now twenty-four and tearful, sitting on the examining room table with no underwear on in preparation for her pre-op genital exam. I reach forward and take the book from the physician, unself-consciously going to cross my legs at the knee before a strategically cool breeze reminds me of my semi-robed state. I am actually smiling at the pictures and diagrams. The physician runs her index finger along the bumpy edges of an illustration of yellow, fatty tissue filled with viscous pus.

"See this is the cyst. Yours is about 3.5 centimeters long. That's about …" She holds up her hand, making an *O* between her index finger and her thumb. "That's about the size of, I don't

know, a large walnut?" I flinch. She redirects and points back
to the book. "We'll send yours to the lab." Tracing little rocky
pebble edges and brown ridges she says, "Some grow hair....
Some even end up growing teeth!" She smiles at me. I return
the gesture self-consciously, looking back at the diagram. After
a few moments she gently removes the book from my hands,
returning it to the bottom shelf of the cart. I lean back on the
table, bend my knees, put my ankles in the stirrups, and the
examination begins.

As I prepare myself for the insertion of the speculum, I feel
the customary embarrassment that this sort of clinical physical
contact alone can inspire. I wonder silently to myself if my cyst
will have hair or a full row of teeth, like a child. I have always
wanted to be somebody's mother, although partnering with
someone for life is beyond the scope of my twenty-four-year-old
understanding. I want to feel my body swell with the expectant
pressure of a growing life, expel it from my passage. I wonder
what the pictures of my insides will look like from the camera
they insert during this type of surgery. They have already taken
so many pictures. The MRI, the ultrasounds, the physical
exams. I wonder how these will be different.

I look at the flat surface of my mons as the doctor continues
her work and wonder if the hair in my cyst will match the hair
on my head or if it will look more like the hair on my genitals.
Or maybe it will look like the hair on my underarms and legs?
Outside of my big hands that I think I inherited from my
grandfather, my hair has always been my secret vanity. I wonder
if my cyst will be blessed with hair and laugh silently to myself.

My mother tells me days after I wake up from surgery that the doctor came into the room to tell us that there was hair in the cyst. I have no memory of this moment, but it still makes me smile. When the doctor later shows me photos of the cyst on a computer screen, I think to myself, "It really was about the size of a large walnut inside the shell." It is the clearest photo I have ever seen of my insides before.

PART III: SOMNILOQUY

"Well Danielle, something *could* happen."

This is what my therapist says when I am thirty-two years old, three years after my diagnosis. I am out in the deep expanses of the woods in the Adirondacks of New York. For two weeks the writers in residence have no cellphone service, but just enough Wi-Fi to work online and to make video calls, if we are sitting in just the right spot. I am taking this call in private (Or at least in the small amount of privacy you can get while living in a communal house in the woods.) I stare at the screen, taking in the image of my therapist's brown face. I blink at her slowly, letting her response sink in. I have just finished telling her that I keep up with my medication every day now. That I sleep better at night and I'm working on my issues in therapy so that I'll never have to go back to the hospital again. I say this last part with a triumphant tone because I so desperately hope against all hope that it will come true.

She goes on to say, "Well, what if you can't pick up medication one day? Or you lose insurance? Life is full of unexpected changes. The best we can do is prepare for them." Now I am truly in a panic. "Prepare for them" sounds oddly

defeatist to my ears. I don't want to "prepare" for challenges.
I want to slay them, conquer them, survive them. I have just
finished telling her that the past four months have been the
happiest period I can remember in my adult life, and this is her
response. "Preparing" seems like something you do when you
know disaster is on the horizon.

Soon after this moment we sign off Zoom. Although I
know this is not her intention, I leave the meeting feeling sorry
for myself and incurable.

Before my therapist pointed out this glaringly obvious
truth about my mental illness, I had fantasized about a day
when I would be "cured" or "fixed." I imagined if I was just
good enough, worked hard enough, tried for long enough, that
I would be healed of bipolar depression. I am now faced with
irrefutable evidence that my hopes are wrong. This diagnosis,
in some ways, dictates the rest of my life. This is not a sprained
ankle or a cold that can be nursed with a cast or hot tea. This
was a part of me, is a part of me, and will remain a part of me
until the day I die.

When other people call me "bipolar" I usually correct
them by saying, "I *have* bipolar depression, I am *not* bipolar.
You wouldn't say to someone 'You *are* cancer' would you?" The
average response to this well-rehearsed and slightly stroppy
speech is an embarrassed apology. The people who I love and
who love me in return want desperately to say and do the right
thing. They have been with me through hospitalizations and
heartbreak, illness and good health. And yet my desire for
correction seems to be as incurable as this disease that rules my
mind.

When I was a child, I used to sleepwalk. Once I woke up in the hallway in my pajamas looking at the face of my confused mother. We locked eyes before I threw up theatrically and inelegantly all over the floor. I had no memory of even leaving my bed. After that, my babysitter at the time was instructed to feed me fewer soft-boiled eggs for breakfast, even though they were my favorite.

Many mornings my mother would report that she heard one of us get up to pee in the middle of the night, even running the water to wash our hands and flushing the toilet. We soon figured out that I was the likely offender, although I'd have no memory of the events. As I grew older, this nighttime sleepwalking evolved into snoring and talking in my sleep. I never revealed anything damning with my somniloquy, mostly sticking to incoherent phrases like, "Did you put the pie in the bank?" or peals of unconscious laughter. Some part of me hoped that my bipolar depression would be like my sleepwalking. That it too would evolve into something I deemed more normal and benign, like a snore.

I close my laptop after therapy and ponder over this old truth that feels new in my body. There is a certain finality in "incurable" that feels rough against my skin, as if it is rubbing the wrong way against the grain. I so desperately want to be cured. I don't even know what "cured" would look like.

After this session, I am afraid because so much of my health depends on the small pink tablets I swallow every day, and the therapy calls I make once a week, and the loved ones with listening ears and open hearts, and the health insurance I get through my job. This careful cocktail of support keeps me balanced and alive. Before my therapist's flat-footed statement, I had dreamed about a day when it wouldn't take quite so much infrastructure to keep me well. I had dreamed of a day when the business of living would be easier when the burden of illness would be lighter, when the joy of surviving would finally set in. Instead, I feel grounded, connected to the universe, achingly human, and desperate to outlive this disease that in reality I never will.

I want to write you a romance of an ending, but the words are jumbled on my tongue like sleep talk. I want to write to you about inspiration and love.

Instead, I offer you the incurable truth of my body.

Small and finite.

Triumphant and scared.

Reaching out for yours.

Acknowledgments

A book is not only the result of an author's effort. Many people and institutions lend their support to the creation of any work and mine is no exception.

I am deeply indebted to the following institutions and programs for supporting the completion of this book: the Tin House Summer Writing Workshop, the Adirondack Center for Writing Anne LaBastille Residency, the Banff Centre for Arts and Creativity Virtual Writing Residency, and the Tin House Seminar program. Each experience contributed immensely to the development and creation of my memoir. I'd also like to thank my residency mates, classmates, and instructors (Kiese Laymon, Moez Surani, and Aisha Sabatini Sloan) at these various programs for their kind hearts and open minds as I worked toward the completion of my manuscript. Their generosity of spirit inspired me and helped me push toward the finish line!

Many thanks are also due to my parents, Ronald and Paulette, who have made me feel cherished and worthy since I was a small child while also giving me the sense that I am capable of achieving my dreams. I would also like to thank my siblings, Brian and Kimberley, who are my dearest friends, confidants, and sources of support through the years. Thank you to my sister-in-law, Becky, for her good humor and light (And for never complaining when Brian and I spoke on the phone for over two hours.)

I am grateful to my friends whose love and dedication have buoyed me through some of the darkest moments of my life. If I call you friend just know that I hold you in my heart in the highest possible regard. You make life wonderful.

Thank you to everyone who has listened/read/revised drafts with me over the years. This book is so much better for your insights and care.

And finally thank you to my partner, Amanda Suckow, for their love, for their belief in me and this project, for always being my first reader … and second reader … and third reader, and for giving me the courage to pick this book up again after many years so that I can publish it. I love you beyond reason, beyond words, beyond the confines of the human heart.